RIDING FOR BEGINNERS

SIBYLLE LUISE BINDER AND GEFION WOLF

RIDING FOR BEGINNERS

STERLING PUBLISHING CO., INC.
NEW YORK

Translated by Elisabeth E. Reinersmann
Edited by Claire Bazinet

Library of Congress Cataloging-in-Publication Data

Binder, Sibylle Luise.
    [Reiten fur Einsteiger]
    Riding for beginners / Sibylle Luise Binder and Gefion Wolf.
        p.   cm.
    Includes index.
    Summary: Includes information on how and where one can learn to ride a horse,
how horses think, the right way to care for and train a horse, and the requirements for
becoming a good rider.
    ISBN 0-8069-6205-4
    1. Horsemanship—Juvenile literature.   2. Horses—Juvenile literature.
    [1. Horsemanship.   2. Horses.]   I. Wolf, Gefion.   II. Title.
    SF 309.2.B555   1998
    798.2—dc21   98–444422
                                            CIP
                                            AC

10   9   8   7   6   5   4   3   2   1

First paperpack edition published 2001 by
Sterling Publishing Company, Inc.
387 Park Avenue South, New York, N.Y. 10016
Originally published in German as *Reiten für Einsteriger.*
Copyright © 1997 by FALKEN Verlag, 65527 Niedernhausen/Ts.
English translation © 1998 by Sterling Publishing Co., Inc.
Distributed in Canada by Sterling Publishing
℅ Canadian Manda Group, One Atlantic Avenue, Suite 105
Toronto, Ontario, Canada M6K 3E7
Distributed in Great Britain and Europe by Chris Lloyd at Orca Book
Services, Stanley House, Fleets Lane, Poole BH15 3AJ, England.
Distributed in Australia by Capricorn Link (Australia) Pty. Ltd.
P.O. Box 704, Windsor, NSW 2756 Australia
Printed in China
All rights reserved

Sterling ISBN 0-8069-6205-4 Trade
                 0-8069-6743-9 Paper

CONTENTS

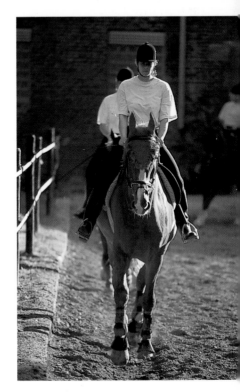

INTRODUCTION

Shouting for joy: Ludger Beerbaum on Sprehe Ratina Z, at the 1996 Olympic Games in Atlanta, after winning the Gold Medal for Germany in the Equestrian Team Event.

Another horseback riding manual? Yes, another one. And what we have to teach is still based on the valid theories of the old riding masters. But the expectations today of those who want to learn how to ride have changed. Now, beginners don't want to have to choose in advance: classic English school of riding or Western's more relaxed, recreational style. Today, happily, we have a number of alternatives available to us.

Horseback riding has changed, especially in the last few years, from an elitist to a popular sport. Recreational riding is done just for the fun of it. So, why shouldn't learning to ride be fun too?

Because of this idea, the way horseback riding is taught has also changed much in the last few years. Still, most standard textbooks still put the skill of thoroughly training horses front and center, no matter how outdated that has become now. Most people aren't interested in learning to train horses. They just want to learn how to ride a horse, for fun, during their time off. Their primary goals are to be safe in the saddle, to feel comfortable, to have good communication with their horse and to be able to keep up with other riders on the trail.

When people who are interested in learning how to ride a horse look for books on the subject, ninety percent of the time they find information that goes way beyond the needs of a beginner and still doesn't fill their special needs.

Horseback Riding for Beginners is designed to fill this gap. Here is valuable information on why, how and where a beginner can learn how to ride a horse. It tells you how horses think, talks about the right way to care for and train a horse and, last but not least, it covers the requirements of beginning riders—what you need to learn in order to become a good rider.

With this somewhat different horseback riding manual as a reference, the reader will be able to go on and enjoy wonderful trail rides, and will know what it means when the instructor says "brace your back," "lower your heels," "do a leg yield," and gives other instructions.

This book is meant for those readers who:

- want to learn how to ride a horse
- are still undecided if and how they want to ride
- are beginning riders and are looking for help in their lessons.

Sibylle Luise Binder and Gefion Wolf haven't forgotten their own beginnings. In addition to presenting necessary theories, they recall amusing anecdotes about painful buttocks and unaccustomed sore muscles. They recount situations when a favorite horse stubbornly got the upper hand, butterflies they felt before their first trail ride, and their struggles with equipment.

With the help of this manual, you

should always be safe in the saddle, and will hopefully have as much fun around horses as I have.

Ludger Beerbaum

Ludger Beerbaum on Rush On

WANT TO RIDE? WHAT'S YOUR PLEASURE?

Long ago, things were much simpler. If you wanted to ride, you'd simply count your money and march yourself off to the nearest riding stable. There, a former cavalry officer would likely put you on a horse already saddled and bridled and begin to teach you how to ride in the voice of a drill instructor. Lessons may not be enjoyable, but you had little choice.

Now, since we do have choices, you need to ask yourself two questions, even before you take a lesson: "Why do I want to learn to ride a horse, and what style is best for me?"

Assume your dream is to compete, wearing topcoat and hat, in a dressage event. Taking lessons in Western riding wouldn't get you very far. If you just want to ride your pony on trails through the woods, a classical dressage course wouldn't help much. Time and money also play a role. If you don't want to compete but simply ride for fun, you'll be more comfortable and happy taking instruction at a stable where recreational riding is emphasized.

FOUR BASIC QUESTIONS AT THE START

1. MONEY

The next time you're around friends or co-workers just mention, but loud enough for everybody to hear, that you're learning how to ride. We'll bet that at least one person will ask if you've inherited money or won the lottery.

Much depends on where you live, but many people today still think of horseback riding as very expensive and see the sport of riding as something that only the "upper class" can afford and take part in. But that's not true. Today, riding is a recreational activity enjoyed by even those with an average income, but there are still costs to consider. Riding clothes and riding lessons are required. And if and when you decide to buy and take care of a horse, it's not something you can do on pocket change. (Because most beginning riders think, or just dream, early on about buying and riding their own horse, we've laid out a checklist opposite to help you determine costs, depending on where you live and the type of riding you want to do. It will give you some idea of what you are getting into.)

But before even considering the purchase of a horse, invest your money in lessons. And when you finally learn how to ride, go on an outing or vacation on horseback. A vacation means leaving everyday stress and responsibilities behind and concentrating totally on your new adventure. While such a vacation can seem a bit scary and rough for you right now, we can almost guarantee you a relaxing time in the company of horses and fellow enthusiasts. If nothing else, your first extended success in the saddle will be a wonderful break from everyday routine. And after all, isn't that what being on vacation is all about?

Horseback riding today is neither expensive nor elitist.

10

COSTS CHECKLIST

Riding "just for fun"—one lesson a week

	per month	per year
Basic equipment "classic English style" (boots, hat, riding breeches, gloves), one-time expense		
Riding lessons (4 x a month)		
Riding club or association fees		

If you can afford more: one lesson a week plus a trail ride

	per month	per year
Basic equipment (see above)		
Riding lessons (4 x a month)		
2-hour trail ride a week		
Riding club or association fees		

Owning and keeping the horse in a stable

	per month	per year
One time expenses:		
Horse purchase		
Basic equipment for the horse (saddle , bridle, halter, stable blanket, grooming tools)		
Basic equipment for the rider (boots, 2 pairs of riding breeches, cap, gloves, jacket)		
Boarding fees		
Farrier (blacksmith) 7 x 12 a year		
Veterinary expenses (immunization, worming, check-ups, etc.)		
Liability insurance for people owning animals		

Costs depend on where you live, riding style, and those "extras" you can't resist. Time for some research.

The most important prerequisite when being around horses: take your time.

2. TIME

What is so absolutely wonderful about recreational horseback riding is that it's so relaxing, but only if you take the time—and time is the one thing weekend riders seldom seem to have enough of.

You might say: "Finding one hour a week—the time you might consider the minimum for beginners—should not be a problem." Well, that's precisely the problem: One hour a week is simply not enough. If you arrive five minutes before your appointed lesson, have a horse already saddled and bridled, take your 45-minute lesson, return the horse to the stable and hand him over to the groom, then one hour is plenty. But then you deprive yourself of one of the most significant aspects of the sport: the joy that comes from being with a horse and the chance to experience riding as more than simply an athletic activity.

Time for Yourself...and the Horse

In other words, take your time. Try to find a stable where, right from the start and under the supervision of a knowledgeable person, you'll be allowed to groom and saddle the horse you will ride during your lesson. Such chores give you a chance to make contact with a delightful animal and learn about his behavior even before you ever climb into the saddle. For your part, your relaxation will begin even before your lesson does.

Also, take time after your lesson to remove the bridle and saddle and, if weather permits and the instructor says it's okay, to walk the horse in a paddock or pasture and let him graze. Talk to him—such communication is fun, builds trust and teaches you a great deal about your companion.

Even though you must add to your actual lesson time the amount of time it takes to get to the stable, don't choose a stable just because it's conveniently close to where you live. It might not be the best place for you. It's important to feel comfortable wherever you decide to ride. If you have a choice between a good stable that is fifteen miles away and one that is not quite as good but right around the corner, choose the one that is farther away.

Learning by Watching

If you have extra time, stay and watch others ride. Horseback riding, it has been said, can be learned only by riding, but that's not entirely true. You can learn much by watching others. Don't pay any attention to other onlookers who make fun of students taking a lesson, as is often the case. These people talk a good streak but usually know very little about riding. And, if onlookers make you anxious by making you think they will make fun of you too when you have your lesson, console yourself with the thought that whenever it's their turn in the saddle, others may criticize them, too. Everyone has the right to make mistakes, and even the right every now and again to feel helpless and foolish in the saddle. It's your right especially, because you are a beginner.

Your Own Horse?

Eventually you'll grow past the beginner stage and may think about owning your own horse. Stop for a moment and realistically evaluate how much time is available to you for that. A horse must be exercised, either by you or by being turned out on his own in a paddock or pasture, at least once a day. One hour of horse care won't do if you, like Gefion Wolf, this book's author, want to keep your horse on your own property. Much more is required of you: feeding and watering, grooming, "mucking" the stall (the term for removing manure and soiled bedding), taking care of the pasture, keeping fences in good repair, buying supplies, and much more. You'll barely get by with fifteen hours a week—and that does not even include riding.

Getting ready for the trail: a pony in English tack (above), a horse in Western tack (below)

More important, you'll first need to acquire the knowledge of horse care that will permit you to keep a horse healthy and happy.

Decide how much you want to invest in the sport in terms of time, energy, and financial and emotional commitment, and then decide how far you want your enthusiasm for horseback riding to carry you.

Jean Claude Dysli of Spain teaching Western riding

3. TALENT

Riding a horse might sometimes also be a question of talent. At least that is what SLB's riding instructor thought, telling her, "A natural talent you are not." Nor did she have a perfect figure for riding, not being "lean, long-legged and very lithe" (this could only be said about Gefion Wolf, who, from a physical standpoint, represents the "ideal" horseback rider).

Not having a natural talent does not mean one has to give up. There are top competitors who would not claim to have a perfect figure for riding. It's rather a matter of how much time and money you want to invest. In the case of the authors: what SLB learned through hard work in the arena and diligent exercises compensated for her less than flexible muscles, even though it often took her several months to learn what came easily to GW. But whenever a horse that belongs to one of their friends develops a problem and is about to get the upper hand, more times than not it's SLB who is asked to come and straighten out the animal and rider.

In other words: don't let anybody tell you that you are not capable of learning to ride a horse. It doesn't matter if you are small or tall, heavy or skinny, a top athlete or a couch potato. Everybody can learn how to sit in the saddle properly, provided that this is what you want and you are willing to invest the necessary effort.

4. STYLE

People ride in two primary styles: English and Western. Western riding did not develop from the European classic style but was the result of the work cowboys had to do in the American West. The philosophy is different: whereas the English rider continuously controls his or her horse to keep the horse in form, the Western rider assumes that the horse brings this form with him naturally; the horse is in a sense more of a partner who is expected to work independently. The difference can be seen clearly when watching an expert rider: the experienced Western rider allows his well-balanced horse to find his own way on a slack rein and only provides supple aids, even when doing spectacular maneuvers. However, the dressage rider always has at least a light contact with the horse and influences every stride.

Before you start your first lesson, take a moment and think about what you really want. Ask yourself: can I dance? Is it easy for me to learn a new sequence of movements and to do them with somebody else? Can I remain relaxed? If the answer is yes, you can assume you won't do badly as an English-style horseback rider.

If you believe you don't have a "natural talent," consider starting out by learning Western-style riding rather than English. This is not to imply that Western riding is easier, but in the beginning the demands on muscles and body control are not as high. In other words, Western riding is an easier entry into the sport.

Both methods have their advantages and disadvantages. Let us compare them and you can make your own decisions as to which style you want to choose.

A Comparison: English or Western		
Consideration	English riding	Western riding
Ability to learn	Takes longer to reach goals like trail riding	Easier in the beginning, becomes "user-friendly" faster
Instruction	Available in all parts of the U.S.	Harder to find in some parts of the eastern U.S.
Versatility	Little or no problem changing to Western riding or other disciplines	Relatively harder to transfer to English riding
Type of horse	Can be done on any type of horse as long as nothing more than average riding is expected	"Classic" Western horses need to be trained to neck-rein
Method of riding	Dressage, jumping, cross country and hunting	Trail riding and Western show disciplines
Comfort	Requires some practice until one feels relaxed and comfortable in an English saddle	Widely considered to be more comfortable for the rider

Once the basics have been learned, English riding is adaptable enough to switch to other styles of riding.

Be clear about the style of riding you want to pursue. Is it the classic English style (here the 1994 Equestrian Team World Champion, Karin Rehbein, on Donnerhall)…

...or rather the Western style (demonstrated by Jean Claude Dysli)?

RIDING: MAKING CONTACT WITH HORSES

The question remains: "How do I find a good teacher and a good riding stable?" Unfortunately, a beginner can't judge from outward appearances if a school horse or instructor is any good. But there are ways to make such a determination.

Generally speaking, trust your intuition or your common sense when you evaluate a prospective stable. Go through the barn and look at the horses. Do they look well cared for, are they gentle, do they let you approach them easily and are they alert and interested? Is the facility relatively clean, light and airy? Observe a lesson: are the instructors interested in their students? Do they explain things well? Do they pay attention to individuals in the group? Do they speak to you in a way you find acceptable? It's important that you feel comfortable in the stable of your choice; after all, you are learning to ride not because you have to but because you want to.

TALL HORSES, SMALL HORSES...

Generations ago, people who rode simply for the fun of it had a much easier time. Horses were everywhere, as cars are today.

Most of us now grow up in cities, and horses are far removed from our experience. Nevertheless, we become fascinated with these creatures—all sizes and shapes of horses.

Ponies and Small Horses

A pony is a full-grown horse that measures less than 14.2 hands at the withers (a hand equals 4 inches; the withers is where the top of the neck joins the body). Pony breeds range in size from the tiny Shetland to the taller Welch and Haflinger. Typical of these breeds are a compact, short-legged body and a sense of independence shaped by their tenacious will to survive.

Blooded and Mixed Breeds

People once believed that a horse's temperament had something to do with the temperature of its blood. For that reason, the huge draft horse with his slow, deliberate temperament and "way of going" was called coldblooded and the lighter and more active Arabian-type was considered hotblooded. When the two types were bred to each other, the result was styled the warmblood, combining the coldblood's sturdiness with the athletic abilities of the hotblood. Thoroughbreds are often referred to as full-blooded, in the sense of "perfectly bred." Controlled breeding has kept their lines well regulated for centuries. These horses are usually destined for the racetrack.

The most popular breeds for American riders are the American Quarter Horse, the Arabian, the Appaloosa, the Paint or Pinto, the Morgan, and the Saddlebred. Pony breeds include the Welch, the Connemara and the Shetland. At riding schools, however, you will most likely encounter the grade, the "mutt" of the horse world. Although a grade is not eligible for a breed registry, that fact does not make the horse any less useful for lessons or recreational riding.

Top: The small version: an Icelandic pony. Bottom, left to right: The warmblood, a Westphalian; compact, an American Quarter Horse; coldblood, a Rheinish-German heavy draft horse

The perfect thoroughbred: Heraldik XX

FROM SLB'S JOURNAL

My First Contact with Horses: Hector, or How I Learned to Take Care of My Backside

One of my very first childhood memories is a vague picture of a very old man sitting on an upside-down bucket in front of a stall. He is gently touching the head of a powerful-looking brown horse. According to stories my parents told us, the old man must have been my great-grandfather, who owned very heavy working horses.

My first memory of a horse, however, is not of one of those battleship-sized creatures, but rather of Hector, a dark brown pony with a rather undefinable heritage: a bit of Icelandic, a bit of... God only knows what. He was chubby and round and with a coat like a teddy bear. I met Hector when I was eight years old and my family was vacationing in the Alps. Soon after our arrival, and to my great delight, I discovered a pony farm next to the inn where we were staying. From that moment on, I was lost to my family, although they could always find me at the stable. And if I wasn't in the stable, I was out in the pasture. Whenever I looked for my parents, it was for one reason only: to make clear that I would be the nicest and sweetest, most perfect child in the world if they would only give me an advance on my allowance for riding lessons. I had discovered happiness on earth in the saddle.

Riding breeches, riding boots, riding cap? Forget it. The first pictures my parents took of me on a horse show me wearing shorts. And I still remember what it was like to feel Hector's coat on my bare legs. Oh, how proud I was.

However, as much as I loved him, Hector had one quirk—he loved the color red. Correction: He not only *loved* red, he was *in love* with it. To this day, I'm unable to explain why and how Hector developed this fondness for my well-padded seat clad in red. But someday I will have solved the riddle and know why Hector not only once but twice nipped my behind. Which, however, did nothing to diminish my love for him.

TALL OR SMALL— THE SAME ANATOMY

A veterinarian named Professor Helmut Waibl begins his "Handbook of Horses" with a beautiful description about equine anatomy: "Only when we understand the structure and function of all his individual organ and body systems will we gain insight into the behavior of a horse, his reaction to the world around him, and the performance we can expect of him."

Although Professor Waibl might be right and although both of this book's authors are experienced riders, having dealt with horses intensively for years we have never tried to memorize a horse's anatomy or the functions of all the organs. We don't believe it's really necessary, especially for beginners. However, a certain basic knowledge *is* useful, so let us look at certain key parts of the horse.

FOREHAND AND HINDQUARTERS

Forehand and *hindquarters* are terms that you will hear throughout your riding career. The forehand refers to the part of the body in front of the saddle. Now, when you are watching a jumping competition, you'll understand that the term "forehand fault" refers to when the horse has knocked down an obstacle with his *front* legs.

The hindquarters refer to the part of the horse behind the saddle. Watching a dressage competition, you can speak like a real pro when you observe:

"This rider has activated the hindquarters." (What it means to *activate* the hindquarters is discussed later in this book.)

MUSCLES AND TENDONS

Horses are made not only of bones but of muscles, tendons and organs. Although it's not necessary to know all of them by name, it is vital to remember that horses' legs have many tendons and, if they are sore or otherwise injured, the result is lameness.

Leg tendons are maintained in good shape by regular exercise. In addition, every rider should make it a habit to check the tendons of the horse's legs after every workout. Ask an experienced horseman to show you how to run your hand over the back of each lower leg. When a horse stands straight and supports his weight over the leg you are examining, the tendons are easy to make out. Normal tendons are small and hard, without any spongy or hard swelling. They will feel cool to the touch.

LUNGS AND DIGESTIVE SYSTEM

Lungs
As the result of their free-roaming life in the wilderness, horses' lungs developed into high-performance organs that are not very resistant to pollution. Dust, dirt and ammonia fumes can damage them.

Horses are happiest outside, grazing in a green pasture.

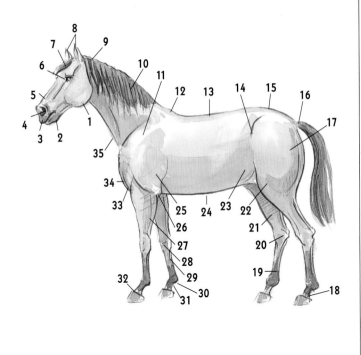

Anatomy of the Horse

1 jaw
2 lower lip
3 upper lip
4 nostrils
5 face
6 eyes
7 forehead with forelock
8 ears
9 poll
10 mane
11 shoulder
12 withers
13 back
14 point of hip
15 croup
16 dock
17 thigh
18 hoof
19 cannon bone
20 hock
21 gaskin
22 stifle
23 flank
24 abdomen
25 arm
26 elbow
27 forearm
28 knee
29 cannon bone
30 fetlock/ankle
31 pastern
32 coronet
33 point of shoulder
34 chest
35 neck

It is therefore the responsibility of humans to minimize such danger by avoiding excess dust inside the stable, regularly and thoroughly mucking out stalls, and not working our horses in a dusty indoor arena but rather allowing them access to fresh air and exercise in a paddock or pasture.

Digestive System

Horses are foraging animals. In the wild, horses for the most part spent their time grazing, continually and at leisure. Accordingly, their stomachs tolerate only small portions at a time. In addition to concentrated feed in the form of oats or pellets, they need roughage like hay or fresh grass.

The idea that "I want to take good care of my horse so I will give it more food" can have dire consequences. Overfeeding a horse not only contributes to obesity, but due to excess protein from grain, it can also cause life-threatening colic and other painful ailments. Those who see the agony of a horse suffering from colic, often simply because of being fed too much concentrated feed, will never want to see that happen again—especially to their own horse.

However, a carrot, apple, lump of sugar or other offered treat is permissible after you have had your lesson—but watch out for sharp teeth as the tempting goodie is lying on your outstretched palm.

THE FASCINATING MIND OF HORSES

What makes horseback riding such a special sport is that the "equipment" is a living being. It breathes, moves, feels...and sometimes has a mind of its own. It brings to the relationship its own experiences. A horse can be temperamental and it has its own way of expressing itself. If we are particularly good observers, a horse gives us a wonderful chance to be part of its world.

WHY HORSES ARE SO DIFFERENT

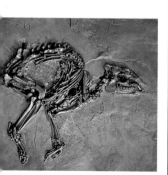

At the museum at Senckenberg/Frankfurt: a fossilized prehistoric horse, found in a cave at Messel near Darmstadt

It's by no means easy to develop an understanding of horses because they react differently from the way we do. They are even different from the pets with whom we share our lives. There is no joyful tail wagging when we approach them, they don't fetch the paper or slippers, they don't purr when we stroke them. And if that wasn't enough, people who ride horses have to listen to some dog or cat owners tell us: "Horses aren't very smart." As proof, they point out that many horses don't even react when called by name (which is true); that it's difficult to train them as we do dogs, who quickly learn to obey a command (also true); that they are not nearly as playful as cats (partly true); and that they don't develop close relationships with people like cats and dogs (not true). But if we really want to decode the behavior of horses, we must first understand that animal and human behavior is influenced by where they came from.

The roots of our social behavior date back to our very origin. So the behavior of horses also stems from influences on the history of their development, a history that started considerably earlier than that of us *Homo sapiens*.

Herd and Flight Instincts

The first horselike being that we know of belonged to the species *Hyracotherium*. These herbivores, hardly taller than cats, roamed the ancient forests 50 to 55 million years ago, hiding from their enemies in thick underbrush. When the increase in the temperature of the Earth's atmosphere turned huge forests into deserts, these early ancestors of the modern horse needed to devise a different strategy for survival.

Hiding was replaced by fleeing. Since timely flight requires vigilance, these animals began to congregate in herds because many eyes and ears could see and hear more than could the senses of a single individual. The need to escape from an enemy quickly also resulted in changes of body structure: the back became longer, the legs became longer, and the legs developed hooves.

Vision

The horse's senses also began to become specialized. Humans in their early history needed sharp eyesight for their hunting and gathering activities, so they trained their eyes to focus straight ahead. However, horses needed a wider view of their surroundings and, therefore, developed the mechanism for greater lateral vision. It was important that a horse be able to detect the approach of enemies from every direction, no matter the position of his body; so his eyes are located further to the sides of his head. Except for a small blind spot directly in front of his head, a horse can see everything around him. But this wide-angle vision came at the expense of visual acuity, or sharpness. In practical terms, this means that if you approach a horse from behind he will be aware that you are there but won't be able to recognize you. A horse most likely sees his surroundings only in shadowy detail.

For that reason, when walking up to a horse, approach slowly and also use your voice. And, if you want a horse to get to know you quicker, try in the beginning to wear the same clothes; since horses recognize not only a face but the whole person, it's possible they think that clothing equals fur. Look at it from a horse's point of view: wouldn't it be hard for you too if your cat or dog changed color and shape every day?

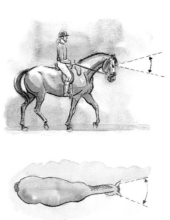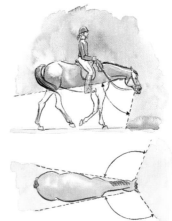

The side placement of the eyes gives a horse excellent long-range vision but also creates a so-called blind spot directly in front, below the nose. The vision close to his sides is also somewhat blurred so, in order to see things more clearly, the horse must lower his head.

THE EARS

The ears also have become specialized. Look at horses grazing in the pasture and watch how their ears move constantly. A horse's sense of personal safety requires a very keen sense of hearing. What is missing in clear vision is made up through sharp hearing. A horse can hear a mouse moving through the brush as well as a member of the herd calling from a long distance.

Ears pointing forward and eyes opened wide, this horse is expressing interest in what is going on.

Consequently, a human's voice can be an excellent aid in many situations. The voice identifies a person and serves to calm and praise as well as reprimand. Don't hesitate to use your voice so a horse can recognize your unique tone. Talk to your horse often when grooming or sitting in the saddle.

HERD ANIMALS AND HIERARCHY

Forget for a moment all the horse movies where wild stallions, with voices sounding like trumpets, corral their timid mares to protect them from danger. Such a well-functioning hierarchy within a herd is more the product of male-idolizing imagination on the part of scriptwriters than an accurate observation of horses in the wild.

The Lady's in Charge

Because life within a herd tends to be quiet and team-oriented, the hierarchy in the herd functions according to a matriarchal system. "The boss of the herd" is not a stallion but a very experienced mare. She has not reached this rank by terrorizing other members but by demonstrating the benefit of her experiences: She has proven that she can find water during a draught, locate green pastures, and sound a timely alert when the herd needs to flee from an enemy.

The Male's Place

The males of a herd can flirt with the mares, graze with them, sire foals and, when situations become dangerous, become protector of the herd. If things become serious, it's the stallion's responsibility to put himself between the fleeing herd and the attacker. While mares and foals flee to safety, the stallion uses his teeth and hooves to teach the attacker necessary respect. However, if he is not successful and a foal is lost, mares terminate their loyalty and search for another stallion who will offer better protection.

Consequences for the Rider

For the rider, this hierarchical structure represents a minor disadvantage but also a very great advantage. The disadvantage comes from a horse's feeling uncomfortable when alone. A single cat is happier than a horse that is kept by himself. If psychological problems, which are usually manifested in various quirks and behavioral problems, are to be avoided, a horse needs to have contact with other horses.

However, because horses are social beings they are willing and able to integrate people into their "world." Even though we neither look nor behave like horses, we are still able to be considered family members. If we go about it in a proper way, we can even become accepted as the highest ranking member of "the herd," even if that herd consists of one person and one horse. If we do it skillfully, we can be the *alpha horse* that other horses listen to, to whom they willingly and gladly subordinate themselves and in whose company they feel safe and comfortable. Every rider would do well to assume that position, if for no other reason than for safety. This is why we should not leave the thinking to the creature with the larger head; it's the rider's job and responsibility to create the trust necessary for a successful relationship.

For horses to be healthy, they need the company of other horses.

UNDERSTANDING HORSES

Imagine waking up tomorrow morning and finding yourself in a country where you neither speak nor understand a word of the language. In addition, you have ended up in a village where nobody speaks English. What are you going to do? Maybe pantomiming would help, if the people are willing to take the time to "read" your body language.

Now, imagine that you are a horse. You do not understand human language and can't speak it. How *can* you communicate?

Do you understand the language of horses?

Actually, understanding the language of horses is not all that difficult. No, we wouldn't put you through a course of whinnying because—in general—horses rarely communicate with their voice. They express themselves in most cases by imitation and using body movement, and people who know how to interpret their moves are halfway home when it comes to communicating with horses. The rest is a only a matter of sensitivity and experience best acquired by just being around horses.

As study objects we've chosen a few photos that show typical, expressive faces as well as the mimic body posture of horses.

"**Thanks, I'm fine. You?**" is what this horse is saying. Ears are pointed in your direction, lips are relaxed. It's the expression of a contented, happy horse who wouldn't mind if you were ready for a bit of conversation.

"**Something interesting is going on over there!**" Ears are pointed in order to hear better; the horse is looking toward the sound. Slightly tightened lips are a sign that the animal's attention is fully engaged.

"I'm so bored, I'm falling asleep" is what this horse is saying, A relaxed body posture often includes one hind leg resting on the edge of its hoof. This horse is dozing. Be cautious when you approach such a horse from behind. Make your presence known before you get close; otherwise if he is startled he could react with a swift kick.

"I've had enough. I'm ready to fight!" This horse is threatening, with ears flattened, lips tight, eyes widened, clearly agitated and with tail swishing. When you see this look, keep your distance and speak calmly (if he's very rambunctious, speak more authoritatively). Wait for the horse to calm down and the ears are turned upright again.

"Ah, it looks like I'm getting some food." This is what a horse looks like when feeding time is near and he is looking for his grain. Sometimes a horse will lick his lips in anticipation.

"Boy, something smells interesting." Here the horse is turned in the direction of an appealing smell, with a raised head, taking deep breaths, and the upper lip pulled up to the nostrils to hold the odor as long as possible. This expression is often a sign that a stallion has caught scent of a mare in heat.

Horses have a lot to say.

EQUIPMENT FOR HORSE AND RIDER

This chapter won't give you an excuse to spend a fortune on clothing and equipment. The authors tend toward "pragmatic minimalism," meaning you buy only what you really need and those items you buy should be made well enough that they will last. Real horsemen don't care much about the latest fads.

However, horseback riding is supposed to be fun. So if you really want to look chic at the stable, and you love the idea of coordinating your horse's tack with your outfit, in colors that are "in," go for it. Just don't look like a bright red fire engine—most horses are irritated by that color. Otherwise, to each his own.

THE RIDING OUTFIT

A SMART RIDER WEARS PROTECTIVE HEADGEAR

To a rider, a helmet is as important as the horse. That's not because, traditionally, a bareheaded gentlemen or lady on horseback was unthinkable. Today, a hat is worn to protect the rider; it doesn't matter if we're talking about a hunt cap, a top hat or derby worn for dressage competition, or a jockey helmet, so long as it has a reinforced shell and shock-absorbing lining and a well-fitting chin strap. The purpose is not to look fashionable, but to protect your head in case of a fall.

Many if not most stables insist that all riders, not just beginners, wear such headgear for reasons of insurance liability as well as common sense. Therefore: a protective helmet is the first thing that you as a riding student should buy. Even Western riders, who traditionally wear felt or straw cowboy hats, now consider hard headgear a sensible idea when they are learning to ride.

Above: Hunt cap; below: Cross-country or jockey helmet

Don't try to save money by using a helmet that has been handed down from your sister, friend, or cousin. A hat that has been kept in the basement for over twenty years and is sliding down over your ears won't do. Neither will one that has been involved in a hard fall where the shell might have cracked. Instead, invest in a new, well-fitted, crush-proof, shock-absorbent helmet with a chin strap, as shown in the photo. These helmets vary in price and style (ventilated models are good for warm-weather riding) and are available in every specialty shop or through tack shop catalogs, whose addresses can be found in riding magazines. If you order by mail, make sure that you submit your correct hat size or an accurate measurement of your head.

A PRACTICAL TIP

SLB Hates Helmets

I don't believe I'm particularly vain, but whenever I try on a hunt cap type of safety helmet and look in the mirror, I automatically think, "My God, how stupid it looks!" Furthermore, most hunt caps are uncomfortable. They pinch, and the dark velvet quickly starts looking dirty and worn when kept either in the stable or a car. That's why riding helmets are not for me.

But since I *am* very interested in protecting my head, I wear instead a military helmet known in the United States as a cross-country or Caliente helmet. These helmets are much more comfortable. If you don't like simple black, use a colorful cloth cover that comes in different designs. It can be easily washed when dirty. These helmets provide as much protection as hunt caps and cost only a bit more. Should you be one of those people who think they look ridiculous in a hunt cap, a military helmet might be your answer.

PARKA, PULLOVER AND SHIRT

We could endlessly discuss the advantages and disadvantages of all kinds of riding clothing, but would be hard-pressed to find a logical reason why a beginner must spend a fortune for them. With regard to something worn above the waist, anything that's comfortably loose and doesn't cause you to perspire after the slightest bit of exertion is appropriate. Layering has proved to be practical: select a jacket or parka that's short enough in the back so you won't sit on it but won't flap in the wind and annoy the horse. Under it you might wear a comfortable sweater and T-shirt of cotton, wool or another natural fiber, or a synthetic material that draws away perspiration. Keep in mind that your instructor will have difficulty judging your posture in the saddle if your clothing is too bulky.

RIDING BREECHES

Real riding breeches are not necessary for the first few riding lessons. Soft, comfortable jeans with smooth inseams (for comfort) work perfectly well. But if you continue to ride, you'll want to think of investing in breeches that won't crease, chafe or ride up your legs. Riding breeches come in two basic models: with knee patches or full-leather seats.

Breeches with Knee Patches
If you sit on the horse properly, riding breeches suffer the greatest wear at the knees; the reason why most come with knee patches. Today, there are many different kinds of knee patches: fabric,

synthetic material or suede leather. We believe that leather is best. In addition to protecting the fabric of the riding breeches, suede leather sticks to the saddle better, which is helpful in maintaining close knee contact.

Whether to choose breeches made of denim, cotton, corduroy or synthetic stretch fabric—or pleated at the waist, checkered, or fancy—depends on your personal taste and budget. Breeches are available in an affordable price range; and you are sure to find an average pair worth your money. For your first purchase, however, stay away from catalog sales. Go to a local store that sells horseback riding apparel and check over what they have. Make sure to find the size that works for you. Don't look for the tightest pair. Tight breeches that pinch in the waist or seat make it difficult to move about and are not a good buy. When trying breeches on, test them. Bend your knees and sit in a chair. Better yet, climb on the wooden horse found in many saddlery shops. If you are comfortable—nothing pinches—you've probably found the right pair.

But, before you decide, do make sure that the breeches are long enough. You'll end up very unhappy if the Velcro closings are in the middle of your lower legs, where they create pressure points, or cause the breeches to ride up inside your boots. On the other hand, breeches that are too long will bunch up around your ankles, which is equally uncomfortable.

A vest with a warm lining: closely tailored without being too tight

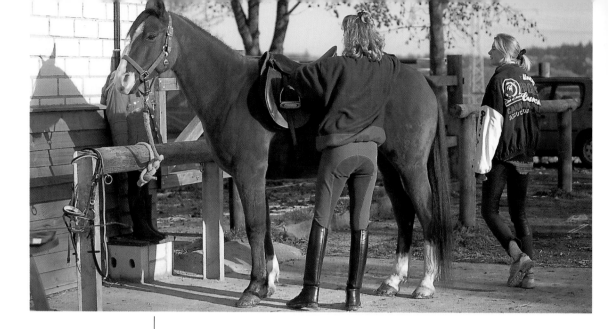

Riding Breeches with Full-Leather Seat

Riding breeches with a full-leather seat have two advantages: they allow you to sit better in the saddle and, if they are properly cared for, they will last longer. Unfortunately, they also have two disadvantages, compared to breeches with knee patches. They are considerably more expensive to buy and slightly more complicated to clean. If you buy full-leather-seat breeches, pay attention to the cleaning instructions that come with them (see also SLB's suggestions on caring for leather-seat breeches). Be particularly sure that the breeches fit well and give it some thought before choosing a fashion color. Consider a neutral blue, gray or green, which will serve you better over time, because the breeches should last for several years.

FOOTWEAR

The choice of footwear depends on your taste and your budget and is a

---

A PRACTICAL TIP

SLB's Care for Leather-Patch Breeches

The full leather-seat breeches I own are washer cleaned in warm water and on delicate cycle using an appropriate detergent. I expect them to withstand that kind of treatment. They are never put in a drier but are rather air-dried. Avoid the bright idea of drying breeches faster near or on top of a radiator. The leather will quickly deteriorate.

Breeches are usually very stiff after drying, and manufacturers suggest thoroughly kneading and massaging the garment. Some people squeeze themselves into newly dried breeches and, after a few hours, their body temperature has made the breeches soft again. That kind of punishment is not for me. After the pants are dry, I turn them inside out and apply a generous amount of Nivea (or other suitable) cream to the inside of the material. You'll be surprised how soft the breeches become; as comfortable as if they were new.

question of comfort. As a matter of safety, shoes or boots must have heels to prevent your foot from slipping through the stirrup. The footwear also needs to be sturdy enough to protect against the damage that a horse's stepping on your foot can cause.

Leather Boots

The best footwear for English riding is classic leather riding boots. They give you proper support and foot position in the stirrups. If spurs are worn, they'll rest in the proper place. Once the boots have been broken in, they are comfortable and will look good. They have built-in reinforcement for safety—very important, as we have said, if a horse should accidentally step on your foot. If properly cared for, a pair of boots will last you long into your riding life. However, good ones are not inexpensive.

Rubber Boots

Rubber boots are a less expensive alternative to leather. Many are made with a leather insole that gives sufficient air circulation and are waterproof. But a word of warning: the boots offer little protection against being stepped on. So, rubber boots are recommended for beginners, who should keep in mind, however, that these very inexpensive boots are really not very good.

Jodhpurs and Jodhpur Boots

An acceptable alternative to high boots and breeches are jodhpur boots and jodhpurs. Jodhpurs were originally developed by the British in India for com-

A PRACTICAL TIP

SLB's Comfortable Boots
If you want a pair of boots to serve you well, they must fit. When they fit properly, they are rather narrow just below the knee. That is why you need a boot hook to put them on and a boot jack to take them off.
    This has always bothered me, and is the reason I went to my shoemaker and asked him to open the rear seam on each boot and put in a zipper. The zippers don't affect my riding, but they have made putting my boots on and pulling them off a lot easier and more comfortable.

fort during warm summer months. However, these type of pants provide little protection for your legs, and if you have particularly sensitive skin, chafing by stirrup leathers can bruise you.

Jodhpurs and low boots are traditional apparel for youngsters, since replacing them when they are outgrown is less expensive than buying new high boots and breeches.

Above: Leather boots
Middle: Jodhpur boots
Below: A complete jodhpur outfit

Chaps

Chaps (pronounced "shaps") are very popular with Western riders as well as with many English riders for schooling and informal riding. They come with or without fringes, in smooth or suede leather and many different

Go West: Long chaps used in western riding are also popular with English riders.

colors. Chaps are worn over jeans or other comfortable pants, thus saving the cost of riding breeches. They are worn with Western boots, jodhpur boots or paddock shoes.

Mini-chaps, which are the height of tall boots, are another alternative to boots and breeches.

Gloves

Some people wear riding gloves as a matter of course (gloves are mandatory in some competitions). Other people, the authors among them, don't much like gloves. The advantage to wearing gloves is that the reins won't slip when your hands perspire or in the rain. Some riders get sores and blisters on their fingers, particularly when the horse is leaning on the bit, and gloves would be a protection. The disadvantage (at least as far as the authors are concerned) is that you lose a certain degree of "feel."

There is nothing wrong with beginners wearing gloves. Some school horses have a tendency to get a hold of the bit, pulling the reins out of the rider's hands. Here, gloves are good protection. Similarly, many a beginner needs to reach for and hold onto the pommel of the saddle or the horse's neck while trying to find his or her seat, and gloves protect against scrapes.

By the way, riding gloves needn't be made of leather. Simple cotton or wool gloves with reinforcement between the little finger and ring finger are less expensive and are easy to wash.

TACK AND HORSE EQUIPMENT

You might ask yourself why, at this point, we would devote space to a discussion of tack, since you are still a long way away from buying your own horse. Although you probably don't own a horse at the moment, you should know about saddles and bridles because you'll be handling them now. Another reason is that you are responsible for checking parts of them whenever you ride.

THE SADDLE

The type of English saddle most often used in riding schools is the all-purpose saddle. It can be used for jumping as well as for dressage. As with any other saddle, it is most important that the saddle accommodate the rider's seat, that the rider's weight can be carried evenly over the whole surface, and that the tree is high and wide enough not to interfere with the horse's withers.

The terms for the individual parts of the saddle are shown in the drawing below.

The Safety Catch

Every time a rider mounts, he or she is responsible for checking the *safety catch*, the hook by which the stirrup leather is attached to the saddle. Whenever you're in the saddle, the catch must always be in the open position. Then, if a rider catches his or her foot in the stirrup during a fall, the stirrup leather can slide out and the rider will not be dragged along.

The safety catch

The Saddle

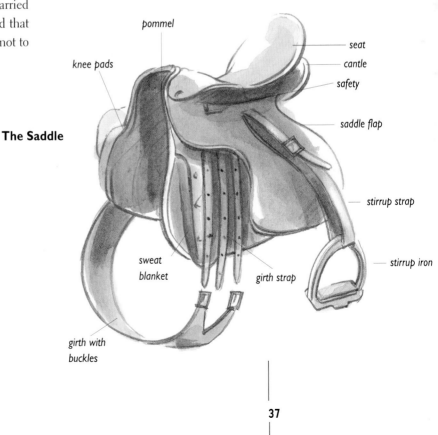

pommel

knee pads

seat

cantle

safety

saddle flap

stirrup strap

stirrup iron

sweat
blanket

girth strap

girth with
buckles

The all-purpose saddle is useful for almost every occasion.

Girth Straps

The second item you have to check regularly is the *girth straps*. As you might have noticed in the drawing on the previous page, there are three straps (called "billets") but only two buckles. The strap in the middle is used as a spare in case one of the others should break. Check all three straps often for wear and tear and don't hesitate to ask that they be replaced when they become frayed.

A saddle should be cleaned after every use with saddle soap (rarely with oil, which makes leather too soft). Somebody in the stable will be glad to explain how riding equipment is cared for and will be very happy to let you practice cleaning a saddle used in riding lessons.

BIT AND BRIDLE

The most often used bit is the snaffle. It is the "mildest" of bits, in the hands of a beginning rider the least likely to cause the horse to be uncomfortable. Snaffles come in different versions; the thicker the mouthpiece, the gentler the bit's effect on the horse. Below are three of them, shown from top to bottom on page 39 on the left: *French snaffle, eggbutt snaffle, double-jointed snaffle.*

At many stables, students are responsible for cleaning the bit of their horse's bridle after a lesson or ride. While you are washing saliva and grass off the bit with clean water, check the joints to make sure that there's no damage.

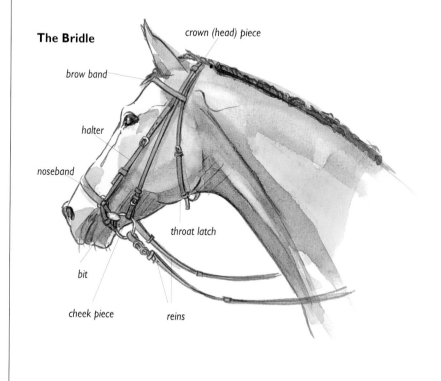

The Bridle

crown (head) piece

brow band

halter

noseband

throat latch

bit

cheek piece

reins

The bit is part of the *bridle*, which also come in many types. The photos on the right show what some look like: From top to bottom: *plain bridle, raised bridle* and *bridle with dropped noseband*.

A patient instructor or groom will give you a lesson in how to take a bridle apart and put it back together again. As you work with the bridle, look at the drawing so you can learn the names of the individual parts. Adjusting a bridle is easy if you have practiced working its buckles and straps beforehand, and you don't want to fuss nervously or unnecessarily around a horse's head.

French Snaffle

Eggbutt Snaffle

Double-jointed Snaffle

Above: Plain bridle

Middle: Raised bridle

Below: Bridle with dropped noseband

HORSES 101: THE BASICS

You arrive at the stable, all decked out and ready to take your first lesson. Is it like learning to drive a car? Not at all. There you slide behind the steering wheel, adjust the seat and rearview mirror, turn the ignition key and learn how to release the clutch without bumping your head against the windshield. However, a horse is more than simply dealing with "one horsepower." Before a horse allows you to sit on his back, and before he does what you ask of him, he wants to know who you are. In addition, he needs to figure out what rank you occupy in his world.

you'll learn little or nothing about how to handle a horse, how to get to know his personality and his needs, and how to deal with an occasional strong-willed animal. But since you may own your own horse someday, you'll need to know much more than how to sit correctly in the saddle. You'll need experience to help you deal with difficult situations. And a good opportunity to get to know your horse and his personality is while you are grooming, leading and walking him.

LEARNING UNDER SUPERVISION

If your stable doesn't provide enough opportunities for interaction with horses, you might consider finding another place. But if your instructor is so good that you don't want to change stables, ask if they might allow you a horse or pony on which you could practice grooming, bridling and saddling, and let you do ground work under the supervision of an experienced person.

YOUR HORSE'S HOME

Horses are for the most part, luckily for them, better off now than in the days when they were simply kept tied up in cramped, narrow stalls. Horses need freedom of movement, even in a shed or stall. You'll most likely find the horse you are to get ready for your lesson in a large box or straight stall, a lean-to or a paddock with access to pasture.

GETTING TO KNOW YOUR HORSE

Some riding stables have personnel who saddle and bridle the horse you will ride during the lesson. Usually, at such places, your only contact with the horse is the time you spend on his back. That doesn't bother most school horses, who really don't care who is sitting in the saddle. They have carried *too* many students through *too* many lessons. Their ongoing contact involves grooms and instructors, and no amount of coaxing, no carrot, no reprimand from a "new" person will impress them.

Those stables that saddle and bridle a school horse prior to your arrival, as a matter of course, might have exceptional instructors teaching the mechanics of horseback riding, but

Always Stay in the Horse's Line of Vision

With halter and lead rope in hand, approach the horse from a slight angle, not from straight ahead. As we have already learned, a horse's field of vision is different from ours. A horse that is approached from the side is better able to become aware of you. If he's facing away from you, with his hindquarters pointed in your direction, speak quietly but clearly and urge the horse to move around to face you or else walk around to his head at a safe distance. This is particularly important when you approach an animal that does not know you.

Greet a Horse as Another Horse Would

Greet your steed in a calm and friendly manner. The deeper and quieter your voice, the better. Pat his neck, let him sniff your hand. And if you really want to do what horses do when they meet each other, gently and carefully blow in his nose. Horses store and remember the scent of other horses, and greeting nose-to-nose is almost like exchanging an olfactory calling card.

Don't hesitate, when you start to put on the halter—do it. Ignore any type of "discussion" or little games. Proceed quietly and with a steady hand, just as you have been taught. This is one of many opportunities to show your horse that it's time to go to work and that you are in charge.

You Are the Boss

Establish right from the beginning that you are the boss, no ifs, ands or buts. Horses are herd animals, organized by nature according to a highly developed hierarchy. If you want to establish a good relationship with your horse, you must behave in a way that fits his world. Horses aren't able, intellectually, to change their innate social programming; because you are the intellectual superior, it's your job to act according to the horse's world and not the other way around.

Approach a horse in the pasture quietly and without distracting movements. Let the horse sniff your hand.

Horses, no matter their size, will fight each other to establish their position within the herd.

HUMAN/HORSE RELATIONSHIP: THE HIERARCHY

How important the role of hierarchy plays has been very graphically described by Dr. Michael Schafer, a behavioral psychologist: "Being ignorant in the way of the world one tends to believe that life in nature is more beautiful and better and, most of all, fairer than in our society...with privileged and less privileged members. However, 'Equal rights for all' does not apply in nature... On the contrary, a very strictly adhered to hierarchy among all social species is the norm—an order that is fiercely and jealously guarded and which is more pronounced than in most human social systems, no matter how conservative they are. This type of strict order gives individuals of lower ranks a sense of security, without oppressing them or making them unhappy, and a respected place within the herd. They know exactly what they can and cannot do."

Establish Your Role Immediately

One of the foremost prerequisites for success with horses involves establishing your position immediately and clearly. As a relatively light and fragile human being, you must always assume the dominant *alpha* role if for no other than safety reasons. Your "partner" brings to any confrontation easily half a ton of weight, and you don't want him pushing you around, even if he is only playing. Also, from the very beginning, you'll want to put a halt to any disrespect a horse might display when he has not yet accepted you as the boss. Therefore, immediately after the initial greeting, establish the roles that he and you will play. If you don't, the horse will do it for you.

Consistency and Dominant Body Language

Dr. Schafer has stated that a "herd of horses is a peaceful social entity as long as the ranks among the individuals have been clearly defined. However, if strange animals are added to the herd...ferocious fights will break out immediately in order to clear any misconceptions about where they belong in that society....Each animal is individually confronted by each other member of the herd, quickly establishing who the dominant member is. This is not necessarily the physically larger, stronger animal but often simply the one which temperamentally possesses superior reflex skills....The fights can be quite violent and sometimes last several days."

This suggests that you needn't look like a weightlifter in order to impress a horse. Consistency, dominant body language, psychological skills and forethought show the horse who is the superior. However, a horse that occupies a high rank in the herd may, in the beginning, try to challenge you.

Earn Respect

Occasionally, especially when a verbal reprimand doesn't work, you need to show more decisiveness. Of course, you should never become abusive. Correction should always be kept to a minimum. Some horses are very sensitive and might need no more than a whip snapped in the air. The more obstinate might need a swift, short tap on their hindquarters. If in doubt as to how to discipline properly, ask someone with experience or get some tips from observing how the "boss" of the herd in the pasture metes out discipline.

Dr. Schafer makes the following observation: "Superiority among horses is asserted by threat without punishment: the superior horse will take the best spot at the feeding trough, is the first to take a dust bath at their favorite spot...and uses very specific body language, like flattened ears, approaching the offender from the flank and raising his tail high in the air. Any horse lower in rank who ignores these signs can expect snapping teeth and kicking hind legs. The respect for a higher ranked horse is so great that fear suppresses any intense desire."

Intellectual Authority

You, as the two-legged *alpha horse*, deserve this respect too. In the same way that the boss of the herd uses physical punishment when everything else fails (but then does not hesitate), deal with your horse first and foremost by using your intellectual authority. In other words, be absolutely clear and unambiguous when you ask something of your horse and then give him a chance to understand what you want from him. If, due to a misunderstanding, you are unnecessarily rough you will only instill fear, which gives the horse grounds to mistrust you. Therefore, in problem situations, make sure first that *you* haven't made a mistake before you discipline your horse.

Prevent any disobedience quietly and consistently by nipping it in the bud. Always praise obedience. Praise is the key to everything, as we are sure you recognize and remember from your own experiences growing up.

Natural authority does not persuade by strong-arm tactics

45

BRIDLING AND LEADING

Inga and her horse Domi demonstrate how a horse is bridled.

Everything that we put on a horse, including the bridle and the saddle, and the way that we lead the animal, is always done from the horse's left side. Mounting and dismounting are also done on the left as military tradition. Cavalrymen in the past had to mount on the left because they carried their weapons, particularly their sword, on their own left side, so mounting or dismounting from the right side would have been awkward. Now, unless you are wearing a sword to take part in a parade, you don't necessarily have to follow the tradition. But in many stables (and of course in horse shows and other competitions) it is considered to be the "correct" way. Some stables that teach Western riding, however, are more flexible, because cowboys often have to work from the right side.

Correct Leading and Tying

The lead rope is fastened to the halter, usually with a quick-release snap or knot, at the ring underneath the noseband. Lead from the left side of the horse and, as you walk, make sure the horse is not moving ahead of you. Remember, you are the "alpha horse"; a "beta horse" knows his place and does not move faster than the boss of the herd and, of course, never walks ahead.

Should your horse be reluctant to follow, encourage him with a gentle pull-and-release series of tugs on the lead rope. Do not pull with constant pressure, because the horse will only pull back against it. Turning towards the horse will only make him tense up and stop in his tracks. When the boss of the herd turns and faces another herd member, it's like a red traffic light: everybody stops obediently and waits until the boss turns around and moves

forward again—the signal to the rest of the herd to follow. That is why it's perfectly normal for a horse to walk behind you when you turn your back to him.

Safety Knot

Tie the lead rope so the horse can't possibly break away, but you can easily loosen the knot if you need to for safety.

One such knot has been proven to be very useful because it can be untied simply with one swift pull. Sailors and mountain climbers know knots that work the same way. While it would be hard for even the most clever equine escape-artist (and there are more than you would think) to undo this type of knot, you can do so quickly. Directions for tying the knot are shown in the drawings to the right. Practice tying the knot so that, when you groom a horse, its use will become second nature.

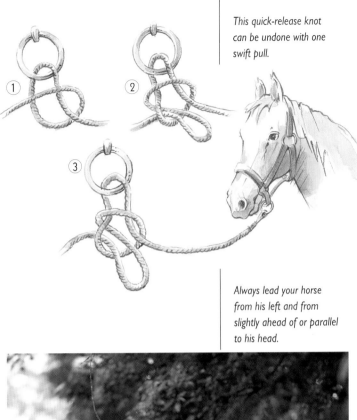

This quick-release knot can be undone with one swift pull.

Always lead your horse from his left and from slightly ahead of or parallel to his head.

Grooming tools (left to right): hoof dressing, hoof pick, applicator brush, plastic curry comb, dandy brush, cloth, sponge, sweat blade, bucket

On page 49, cleaning hooves: Slide your hand down to the fetlock and apply light pressure there, while using encouraging words to convince the horse to lift his hoof. Then you can comfortably scrape the underside with the hoof pick.

CLEANING TOOLS

A well-equipped grooming box should consist of:

Curry combs: a plastic one to remove mud and dirt from the coat; a metal one for cleaning brushes.

Two dandy brushes: a large brush for the horse's body, and a smaller and softer brush for the face.

Hoof pick: to remove embedded dirt from the bottom of hooves.

Sponge: to clean the horse's face.

A stiff bristle brush: to remove dry mud from the legs.

Mane brush: with firm bristles to comb tail and mane.

Soft towel: for drying.

Sweat blade: to remove excess water after washing or shampooing.

Hoof dressing: or hoof balsam, to lubricate dry hooves.

GROOMING

The three classic grooming tools—curry comb, brush and hoof pick—will get your horse clean only if you groom him daily and then only when he is not very dirty or rarely kept outdoors.

Ideally, your horse should have daily access to a pasture for exercise and a "dust bath." Rolling in dust is one of a horse's favorite pastimes, and almost all horses will do it if given the chance. And, if your horse rolls or is otherwise very dirty, you'll need to have the additional tools listed on the left.

Scratching Promotes Bonding

Grooming your horse is not only a matter of hygiene. Brushing also stimulates blood circulation; and it has a social purpose, too. Horses groom each other (we call it "hair-scratching") to strengthen their relationships. If you are a good "hair-scratcher," you'll gain stature in your horse's esteem.

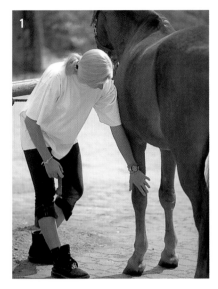

Proper Grooming

How thoroughly to groom depends on how and where the horse is kept. Horses that live primarily indoors have less opportunity to care for their coats and need to be groomed more thoroughly. Horses kept outdoors need to have only the rough surface dirt removed, not the coat's natural protective oil. Only the face and the places where the saddle and the girth come into contact with the body need to be cleaned thoroughly.

Cleaning the Hooves

When grooming, always stand at an angle to and close to the horse, because even the most gentle animal might occasionally strike out—forward or behind with equal force. Start by asking the horse to lift his hoof and, using the hoof pick, remove embedded manure, soil and stones. Dry hooves need hoof dressing (use sparingly), but don't apply at the start of a ride because dirt and debris will stick to the coated hooves.

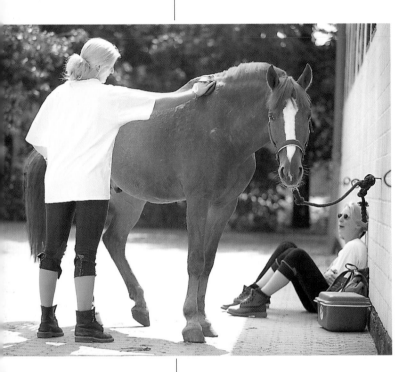

in the direction of the growing coat, cleaning the brush with the metal comb often.

Use a tail brush on a thick mane and tail without breaking and pulling off any of the hair. If the mane and tail are not very thick, you can use a mane comb. Sometimes you will have to separate snarled mane and tail hair with your fingers.

Brush the coat with sweeping motions. Clean the brush frequently with the metal or plastic curry comb.

Curry Comb and Brush

Next, use the plastic curry comb. Hold the comb in the hand that is closer to the horse: your left hand when you are on the horse's left side, and your right hand when you move around to the horse's other side. Always work from the neck of the horse toward his back end. First loosen the caked-on dry mud, where it has accumulated on the body. Tap the curry comb often to remove the dust that sticks between its teeth. Then use a soft brush for the legs. Now switch to a body brush, and again, using sweeping motions, brush

A stiff bristled brush for rough dirt

Even long, matted hair can be smoothed out using a tail brush.

With Sponge and Towel

If necessary, gently clean around the eyes and nostrils with a damp sponge. Don't use a brush or cloth on the insides of the ears, but carefully remove any caked-on dirt with your fingers. Because horses can strenuously object to having their genitals cleaned, you might leave that chore to a more experienced person. If it's your responsibility, gently use a separate damp sponge.

Finally, gently clean the head with a soft brush or a terry cloth, and all that remains is a good clean-up of the area where you have groomed the horse.

AFTER EXERCISING

After a workout, check hooves and tendons for any soreness or injuries. In the summer, when the horse's coat is able to dry in the sun, wash off any sweat from under the saddle and on the neck. Use clean warm water to which you can add a splash of apple cider vinegar; this will restore the natural acidity of the skin (vinegar also works as an invigorating bracer). Remove any excess water with the sweat scraper blade.

The legs also need cleaning, but do not use the vinegar solution on the sensitive genital area. A watering can and a sponge work well here. We don't recommend using a garden hose that delivers a hard stream of cold water: cold water will constrict blood vessels that are warm from exercise.

Always Turn Toward the Gate

When you return your horse to his corral or pasture, before you give him his treat and take the halter off, always turn him towards the gate. If you don't, he might simply take off and start a bucking routine, and you would not be the first person to receive an unintentional kick.

Give him his treat while he is facing the gate, and only then remove his halter. That will give you enough time to step back while the horse is turning around. And, should he decide to entertain you with some enthusiastic acrobatics, you'll be safely out of his reach.

In the same way, when returning your horse to his stall, turn him towards the door before you remove his halter. Otherwise, he is likely to pull you towards his feed bin.

After a shower, remove excess water with a sweat scraper.

Bridling: After the halter has been removed (1) hold the bridle with your right hand at the head piece (2) and with the left hand insert the bit (3 and 4). Once the bit is in the mouth, lift the head piece over the ears (5), and pull the forelock hair over the brow band (6). Then buckle the throat latch (7) and the noseband (8).

A properly fitting bridle has room for your hand to fit between the throat latch and the neck and at least two fingers between the noseband and the face.

BRIDLING

- The horse is standing quietly in the grooming stall. Unbuckle the halter and rebuckle it around his neck. With the bridle in your right hand, stand on the left side of the horse, beside his head. Slip the reins over his head, letting them rest on the neck.

- When closing the nose band, allow enough space for the width of two fingers. When closing the throat latch allow enough space for your fist to fit between the latch and the throat.

- Now remove the halter, take the reins from the neck and hold them together with your right hand below the horse's mouth — but not too far away so that you won't lose control of the horse. Hold the ends in your left hand.

- Should the horse grow unruly, you can always let go with your right hand and still keep control because your left hand is holding the ends of the reins.

- A long whip held in the left hand keeps your horse at a safe distance from you; the whip can also be used to give the horse a little encouraging tap if he walks too slowly.

Horses Like to Graze

If you would like to give your four-legged friend a chance to graze while on a trail, you might leave the halter in place and put the bridle over it. The lead rope can be loosely tied around the horse's neck so you don't have to fuss with it on the trail. Then, when you stop for a while to rest or maybe for lunch, remove the bridle and use the lead rope to tie the horse while he grazes.

Never Wrap the Lead Rope Around Your Hand

Never, *ever* wrap the lead rope around your hand in the mistaken belief that you will have a more secure grip. In the event your horse shies, he can pull with enough strength to really damage your hand.

A PRACTICAL TIP

Teaching While Walking

The more time you spend with a horse, walking in a pasture or grooming or just being around him, the more you will learn about his character, his likes and dislikes, and the more opportunities you'll have to practice establishing your order in the "herd." That training begins when you lead your horse. Teach him to follow you obediently from the moment you take the first step and to stop when you do. Make sure that he does not push against you; insist on your distance. As the top "alpha" horse, you are entitled to your space, and the "beta horse" has no business being in that space. And no matter how appetizing a particular patch of grass may look, never allow your four-legged companion to pull the lead rope out of your hand. He should start grazing only when you say so.

This work-in-hand is a wonderful opportunity for training and exercising. But a more detailed discussion about ground work would go beyond the scope of this book. If you are interested, ask your instructor or a tack shop owner to recommend a good book that deals specifically with this subject. There are many of them on the market.

SADDLING

Your saddle should fit not only your horse but you. If the seat is too big or too small, you can't expect to have a secure seat. Saddle flaps must extend below the knees and not interfere with the tops of tall riding boots.

When you are ready to saddle the horse, be sure that the horse is tied securely to a post or fence. If it has already been bridled, put the halter back on.

How to Carry a Saddle

When you pull the saddle off the rack, place it over your left arm with the pommel at your elbow. Make sure the saddle pad or blanket is securely attached, the girth is draped over the seat and not dragging on the ground, and that the stirrups are pulled up (photo left above).

The Martingale

If you use a running martingale, an auxiliary rein that prevents the horse from raising his head too high, place the strap around the horse's neck without catching it in the lead rope.

Saddling with a Martingale

- Standing to the left of the horse, lift the saddle onto the horse's back and place it slightly ahead of the withers. Then gently slide the saddle back until it's in the proper position behind the withers. Always move the saddle in the direction of the growing hair and make sure the saddle pad is lying flat underneath the saddle (1, 2).

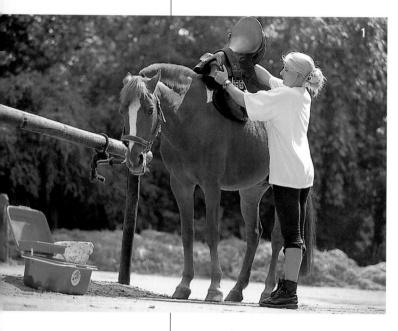

- Now let the girth fall and hang down on the horse's right side. Without hitting his legs, pull the girth underneath his belly and through the loop of the martingale. Then buckle the two outermost billet straps of the girth underneath the left saddle flap (3 to 7).
- Unbuckle the reins and feed both of them through the martingale rings. Re-buckle the rein and you are finished.

Leading a Horse with a Martingale in Place

One slight disadvantage to a running martingale is that you cannot pull the reins over the horse's neck to lead him. Instead, hold them in your right hand as shown in the top photo.

Removing the Saddle

To remove the saddle, unbuckle the girth strap and carefully let it slide to the ground without hitting the horse's legs. Unbuckle the martingale, which usually remains attached to the bridle. Holding the saddle with both hands at the pommel and the cantle, pull it off the horse carefully and place it over your arm. With your other hand, place the girth across the saddle.

Above: Domi with martingale

Left: The girth is pulled through the loop of the martingale.

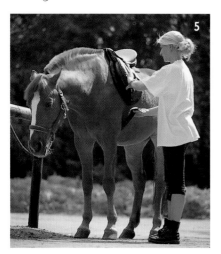

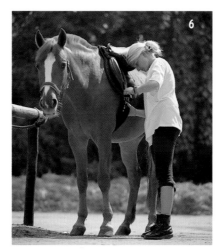

LEARNING
TO RIDE

Most European and some American instructors who teach English riding give beginning lessons on the lunge line. They believe that it is the only way a new student will learn a proper seat and acquire the necessary confidence. Then, after lessons on the lunge line, the student can go on to group lessons and finally, once the student has enough balance and confidence, he or she can leave the arena and ride on a trail.

Many if not most American instructors, however, don't use this lunge-line technique. You might want to discuss the subject with your instructor and see if this method might be useful in your case.

ALONE ON THE LUNGE LINE

If you decide, after reading the section below, that the lunge line method would be best for your first attempt in the saddle, you're in good company. Recruits at the Spanish Riding School in Vienna, leaning how to become riders and trainers, start out that way.

ADVANTAGES AND DISADVANTAGES

One advantage of lunging: it's not easy for novice riders to coordinate their movements with that of a horse in motion. Often they have trouble just trying to figure out what to do with their hands and legs and how to stay in the saddle. If that isn't enough, beginners also have to make sure that the horse moves at a proper speed and correct gait. Starting on the lunge line puts the riding instructor in control so that students can concentrate on what to do with their bodies.

Individual Attention at the Start

As a student on a lunge line, you'll have the full attention of the instructor, who will make sure that no mistakes creep in to spoil learning a correct seat. This is important, since it is easier to correct a mistake at the start—"nip it in the bud"—than after it has become a habit.

Another advantage to starting on the lunge line is that anxious and timid beginners usually feel a lot more comfortable. Knowing that the instructor controls the horse allows them to relax; they don't need to be afraid that the horse will spook because of something they have done wrong.

The Matter of Cost

Two disadvantages to lunging are worth discussing here. The first is that such lessons are more costly than group rates. But here the riding instructor is concentrating on you alone, and the horse will work harder than he would in a group lesson.

Developing a Feel for Riding

The second disadvantage is, in a way, more important. A 45-minute lesson exclusively on the lunge line is a lot of work. The riding instructor is concentrating exclusively on you, and in turn you are concentrating on his or her instructions. After a long lesson, you might suddenly realize that you had no chance for real contact with the horse at all. You were constantly listening to your teacher and didn't really get a feel for the work you were doing on the horse.

Is Lunging What You Want?

The decision of whether or not to start on the lunge is one for you and your instructor to make. If you're willing to suffer sore muscles and sweat because you want to get past the beginner's stage quickly, then starting on the lunge line may be a good idea. But if you prefer to take things easier, there are many training methods that you might find more comfortable.

Lessons on the lunge line will get you over the beginning stage faster.

IN A GROUP

A lot of people don't think much of group lessons. They may say you won't learn much in a group lesson, that individual lessons are easier and better.

In Europe, a "group lesson" means that the school horses work one behind the other. The first rider at the head of the column is the most experienced and the best trained of the group. He works the hardest: he must understand and follow the commands of the riding instructor. The rest of the group can stay more or less relaxed because, since horses are herd animals, they can rightly assume that their horses will "follow the leader." This can make it harder for the "followers" to really learn. However, a good instructor knows his charges and will often have everyone perform the same maneuver at the same time.

The Advantages

Beginners have a chance to concentrate on their seat, and they can assume that their horses are less likely to misbehave during the lesson. Group lessons also cost less than private lessons, the pace tends to be more relaxed, and you'll have a chance to learn from watching others ride.

The Disadvantages

In addition to the absence of one-on-one instruction, a member of a group may have difficulty knowing if his or her aids have caused a certain action or if the horse simply did what the other horses were doing.

FROM SLB'S JOURNAL

My First Riding Lesson

My first lesson was a group lesson. My riding instructor was Alfred Casper, an outstanding horseman, and the horses I was introduced to were all bred and specially trained by him. He knew every hair on their bodies and directed them with only his voice.

When I arrived at the stable for my first lesson, I was told to groom and saddle the horse I was to ride. Her name was Ankara. She was a wise, experienced and very obedient school horse. Then I found myself in the riding ring, standing in the middle of the arena with the rest of the class, for my first lesson on how to mount a horse and sit in the saddle. The instructor then tied my reins together and told me to hold on to the pommel. Off we went. When the rider in front of me turned his horse and walked to the outside track of the arena, Ankara followed her herd instinct and did it too.

When the instructor gave the command "Trot," Ankara trotted obediently. The instructor kept telling me what I had to do and correcting me when I did things wrong. When he noticed that my face was glistening with perspiration and I was getting more and more tense, he simply called out: "Ankara, over here." My trusting little mare obediently marched to the center of the ring where the instructor gave her a treat, while I was allowed to catch my breath, receiving a few comments and explanations in the process.

This is how I completed my first riding lesson in peace and an ever-increasing trust in my horse.

I never became a highly accomplished horseback rider, but I know how to sit in the saddle relaxed and in balance. I am forever grateful to my instructor for letting me find my way in the saddle without overtaxing my abilities.

A good instructor is always willing to help when you get into difficulty.

SECRET: MIXING TECHNIQUES

The best way to learn to ride is a combination of all that we have discussed so far: starting on the lunge line, then in a group; or starting in a group, then learning the finer points of the seat on the lunge line; then going back to group lessons and then possibly alternating between group and individual lessons. This way you'll not only have a chance to become a good rider but will also have fun during your lessons right from the beginning. You won't come under more stress than you can handle but make steady progress.

GYM WORK: OFF AND ON HORSEBACK

If you were never particularly excited about phys ed class, if doing toe touches and shoulder stands are not your idea of fun, you may look at this chapter and say: "They can't be serious! I need to exercise to ride a horse?"

Well, you're in good company. It would often take coaxing to get the authors into a gym, too. But not being in good physical shape has its consequences. Being out of shape, in fact, guarantees that you'll be very sore when you are finished riding (and your "flopping around" up there won't be much fun for your horse, either). That's why exercising will help you to enjoy the good times that are ahead. And we promise to treat you gently.

AT-HOME EXERCISES

Get into some comfortable clothes that don't restrict your movements and then start with stretching exercises on the floor. Stretch both arms and both legs. Close your eyes, but don't fall asleep—relaxation requires concentration. That's not a paradox; *consciously* relaxing them is the way to loosen your muscles.

RELAX

Why relax? Because tense muscles are why you and your horse experience pain and why you end up with sore muscles. A good horseback rider has a well-developed sense of control of his or her body. Someone who has supple muscles can follow a horse's movement with less resistance and won't bounce very much in the saddle. Bouncing places stress on muscles and creates less lactic acid. A rider must also be able to consciously relax his or her muscles in an emergency.

If you are familiar with Tai Chi or any other self-relaxation exercises, you can use those methods. If not, have fun with what we are about to suggest to you.

Even a very relaxed trail ride at sundown requires a rider who is physically fit.

Relax Your Shoulders

Lying down comfortably, start from the top. Try to be conscious of your shoulders. Can you feel your individual muscles? In the beginning, you will need to move your muscles slightly to become aware of them: tense your left shoulder and then your right shoulder once or twice, tightening the muscles as much as you can. Now, let go. It works best if you inhale deeply with the muscles still tensed and then exhale slowly and deliberately, letting the muscles just go limp.

Relaxing the Arms

Now work on your arm muscles: inhale, tighten the muscles in your upper arm, become aware of them. Then exhale while relaxing this muscle group. Continue with your lower arm, and then go on to your hands until you have the feeling that this part of your body is truly relaxed.

Stomach and Pelvis

Now work with your stomach and pelvic muscles. Relax your seat muscles. Place your hands under your seat bones and relax the muscles. You should feel the pelvic bones by becoming aware of their outline. These two bones will eventually find a very comfortable place in the saddle, comfortable because their surrounding muscles provide the "cushion." But they can only do that when they are relaxed. If they are tensed up, they work in opposition to the hard saddle, pounding against it rather than filling it. Ideally, neither your seat nor your horse's back should suffer and become sore.

Leg Muscles

Next come your legs. The thigh and lower leg muscles must learn how to become relaxed and supple. The strength you'll need is created by controlling these muscles. But remember, it takes time and concentration to learn to successfully reach a relaxed state.

Growing "Heavy and Warm"

Imagine your arms and legs becoming comfortably heavy. Deep relaxation makes you aware of the power of gravity. You actually feel the weight of your limbs. Now imagine that your arms and legs are becoming comfortably warm. The arteries widen, your blood circulates more easily. You actually feel the warmth.

Use these exercises to relax the muscles in every area of your body. If you are not quite there yet, work on one area at a time. Let peacefulness and quiet surround you. In time you will be able to relax your whole body.

ONE SMALL PIECE OF ADVICE

If you don't want your family or friends to break out in fits of laughter, do the following exercises when you are alone. When we ride a horse we use muscles that are normally inactive, so the relaxing exercises that are specifically for riding look quite funny to those who don't ride.

Warm up before you start, maybe by walking or running in place for five minutes.

FROM SLB'S JOURNAL

What does a dentist have to do with horseback riding?
I have to admit I was a real coward with a very well-developed dental phobia. One day I was rescued when a friend gave me the telephone number of a dentist who used hypnosis when treating his patients. I was skeptical, but remembered well my previous painful dentist appointments so I was willing to give it a try.

I made an appointment and, a scared and perspiring bundle of misery, I sat in what I have always considered a torture chair. The good doctor, whom I considered a hopeless optimist, told me to relax. Me? Relaxe in a dental chair? Why not put me on the executioner's block?

But the good doctor was unimpressed. Playing comforting music, he told me in a calming voice that he would do nothing that I was not prepared for. The relaxation exercises began and I came through with flying colors, learning so much from the experience. Now I can not only sit in a dental chair and be completely relaxed, but I can do so in any chair in the office *and* in my saddle. Whenever I sit in the saddle and feel an old shoulder injury or a sore knee begin to hurt, I ask my horse to walk and I relax the affected muscles. The pain is stopped before it even starts!

My advice to the people who, like me, tend to be very tense, is, take the time and trouble to learn relaxation techniques. Countless books are available on the subject. Take a class that teaches these techniques. You will be doing yourself a favor, and not only as far as horseback riding is concerned.

The muscles in your lower abdomen are going to hurt because they are not used to this. However, you will be using these muscles when riding, and the more you use them the stronger they will be. But, in the beginning, don't overdo the exercise. Torn muscles are not what we are after—the purpose now is simply to stretch them slowly and gently.

EXERCISE 2:

Exercising the Back Muscles

This exercise should be really fun for people who were told as youngsters not to tip their chairs, because we are asking you to do just that. Find a stool or a chair without a back rest. Sit on the edge with your feet flat on the floor and slightly apart. Since you have learned to use the muscles in your back during the relaxation exercises it should be no problem for you to tighten them now (keeping your back straight). Push your pelvis forward, tilting the stool. This same movement you did as a child to "pump" or start a swing is exactly what you do when the riding instructor tells you to "brace your back." And it is also the movement that gives your hips an elastic spring when trotting.

Exercise 1:

Stretching the Abductors

Women have been taught to always sit and stand with their legs together, because this is "how proper young ladies behave." Now you women (and you men too) have permission to be "improper." Sit on the floor with the soles of your feet touching, using both hands to pull them towards your seat. Your upper body must remain absolutely straight. This exercise is easier to do when you sit with your back against a wall for support. From this position, try to push your knees to the floor with your hands.

EXERCISE 3:

Stretching Shoulders and Arms

Anyone who never sat on a horse with tense shoulders really doesn't know how many muscles we have there, and is probably not aware how tight these muscles can become. That's why riders need to do the following exercise frequently: While sitting or standing, cross your arms and put the palms of your hands together. Now, move your arms upward and back, keeping your palms pressed together tightly.

Back-bracing exercise is best practiced on a stool.

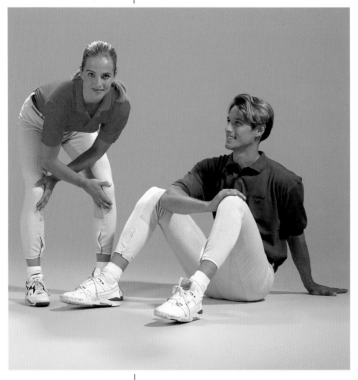

EXERCISE 4:

Strengthening the Seat Muscles

Strong back and seat muscles are needed whenever a rider uses aids to communicate with the horse. The following is a simple method to exercise these muscle groups.

Lie on your back and pull your legs up. Keep your feet flat on the floor and your arms next to your body, straight with palms down. Now lift your pelvis until your shoulders and knees are in a straight line.

EXERCISE 5:

Strengthening the Abductors

You will hear it many times over: "Don't just sit there—ride your horse *actively*." "Actively" means the rider's lower legs must give the horse the aids for constant forward impulsion. This requires strong abductor muscles.

The following exercise is good to strengthen your abductor muscles. Start by bending your knees. While you are bending forward, cross your arms and place the palms of your hands on the inside of each knee. Your upper body should remain straight, with your feet about shoulder-width apart. In this position, push your knees against the resistance of your hands. Your arms may be so strong that any movement is almost imperceptible.

A variation: sit on the floor, pull your legs up and place the lower part of one arm between your knees. Your toes are slightly raised. Now, try to push your knees together against the resistance created by your lower arm.

EXERCISE 6:

Stretching the Calf Muscles

In order to have a rider's low heels and lengthened legs, you need to exercise the back muscles of the lower legs and make them supple. Assume the position shown in the photo above right. Raise the heel of your back foot. Keep your upper body absolutely straight and bend forward, supporting yourself by placing your hands on the thigh of the bent leg. From this position, push the heel of your back foot flat against the floor. The greater the distance between your bent and straight legs, the longer you will stretch.

EXERCISE 7:

Stretching the Muscles in the Lower Legs and Feet

Another particularly important area to exercise for suppleness is your ankle joints. They need to be supple because they provide the impulse for the posting trot and serve as "shock absorbers" when you land after a jump.

It is important to do this exercise in bare feet. Sit on the floor with your legs spread straight out. Rotate your feet in large circles, increasing the effectiveness of the rotation by flexing and stretching your toes. Circle your feet in both directions. Hold your upper body upright.

A variation: pretend that your foot is a paint brush or pen and you are painting or writing. Those who can write the sentence "I do like exercising after all" will be allowed to stop exercising and start riding.

A PRACTICAL TIP

Exercises Done Properly

- Before you start, read the complete instructions.

- The final position of all stretching exercises is held for 10 seconds, all strengthening exercises between 3 and 5 seconds.

- Let the muscles relax between each stretching exercise but not between the repetitions of the strengthening exercises. Let the muscles relax completely only after you have finished a series or a set of exercises.

- At the beginning, do 3 to 5 repetitions of the strengthening exercises on each side. Increase up to 10 repetitions for each side.

- Repeat each stretching exercise 3 times for each side.

EXERCISES ON THE HORSE

Raising your arms at your sides and taking your legs out of the stirrups is one way to learn quickly how to follow a horse's movements in balance.

A word before we begin: get used to the idea that you may look a little strange doing exercises on a horse. It's not something that people often see, so don't be surprised at a few smiles at your expense. But there's nothing better to get you acclimated to being in the saddle, and that's what you want to do—as quickly as possible—so just grin and enjoy it!

Try a few exercises on the follow-ing pages, as demonstrated by Ludger Beerbaum. At the start it's best to do these exercises on the lunge line. Once you have gained more confidence, do them on your own in the indoor arena where you can concentrate.

To prevent losing the reins, tie them together and place them on the neck of the horse. Better yet, ask some-body to lead your horse, at least until you are more experienced.

EXERCISE 1:

Activating the Body and Shoulder Muscles

Raise your arms and rotate them first clockwise and then counterclockwise, keeping your arms close to your body. You can increase the degree of difficulty of this exercise by rotating your arms in opposite directions.

• Rotate 10 times in each direction.

Exercise 2:

Stretching the Hip and Knee-Extensor Muscles

Grasp your left foot and pull the lower leg as close as possible to your seat. Use your stomach muscles to keep your pelvis upright. For safety's sake, take your right foot out of the stirrup.

- Hold each position 3 times for approximately 10 seconds. Repeat with the right leg.

Exercise 3:

Stretching the Flexor Muscles of the Hip

Grasp your left knee with your left hand and pull your leg as close as possible to your upper body. Don't bend forward but remain upright. For safety, remove your right foot out of the stirrup.

- Hold for 30 seconds, 3 times each. Repeat with the right leg.

Exercise 4:

Stretching the Muscles of the Lower Leg

Lift your seat out of the saddle so that your entire weight is in the stirrups. Keep the stirrups right under the balls of your feet. Sink, letting your weight push your heels down and stretch the muscles of your lower legs.

- Hold each stretching position 3 times for 10 seconds.

EXERCISE 5:

Activating the Upper Body and Shoulder Muscles

Alternately stretch each arm as high as possible, reaching for imaginary apples in the air. Imagine that this exercise is pulling your upper body upward.
• Reach up with each hand 10 times.

EXERCISE 6:

Additional Exercise to Activate the Upper Body and Shoulder Muscles

Slowly bend your upper body from an upright position, first forward and then to the side. Then touch the tip of your left boot with your right hand. Using your pelvic muscles, slowly straighten and reach for the tip of your right boot with your left hand. Hold the tip of each boot for 5 seconds. If you can't reach the tip of your boot at first, go as far as you can, maybe to your shin bone.
• Do each side 10 times.

At the very end of these sets of exercises, ask your riding instructor if you can ride your horse bareback at a walk for a few minutes. Riding bareback gives you the closest possible contact with your horse and a better feeling for his movement. The experience is valuable for when you are back using the saddle.

WALK, TROT, CANTER—AND CORRECT SEAT

The time has come for the real thing. But if you thought all you have to do now is sit comfortably in the saddle and let the horse do the rest, you are mistaken. On the contrary, horseback riding is pure movement. Mounting a horse is relatively easy, since under normal circumstances the horse will stand in place quietly. But once he and you are in motion, you must move in unison with your horse. And it's not all that simple.

FIRST THINGS FIRST: MOUNTING

The first time you find yourself standing next to your horse and look up at the saddle, you might wish you had a ladder. "How will I ever get into the saddle?" you may ask. Never fear, there is a way.

DOING IT RIGHT

In most stables, your horse will be led up to you. While it is fairly certain that, as a beginner, you'll be assigned a horse that will stand quietly while you mount, you should know that there's no *guarantee*. A horse will sometimes get scared and take off!

Also, if you are unsure and move too slowly for the horse, he may just take it into his head to wander off. In the beginning, someone will very likely hold the horse's head while you mount, and possibly also the right stirrup, to help keep the saddle centered and in place. But it's important not to dawdle when you mount. With one foot in the stirrup, you're very vulnerable if the horse should move. When you are ready, insert your foot in the stirrup and, as if in one motion, climb aboard.

Check Bridle and Girth Strap

Before getting on, take a quick look at the bridle and make sure that all the buckles are properly fastened. Then check the saddle's girth strap. Usually a horse "blows up" his belly after being saddled to try and reduce the girth's pressure, and it's your responsibility to re-tighten a loose girth.

Adjusting the Stirrups

Pull a stirrup iron down and stretch it alongside your outstretched arm. The length is approximately correct if the iron is level with your armpit. Do this with both stirrups, since they need to be equal in length. Then (and this tip comes from SLB) make sure that the stirrup buckles are slid back underneath the saddle flap; a buckle halfway down your leg will pinch your thigh.

Make these adjustments before you mount. It is difficult to organize and properly adjust stirrup straps when already in the saddle.

Mounting

Some stables have mounting blocks that permit riders, particularly small or elderly ones, to get into the saddle easily. Other stables permit "leg-up" boosts. But everyone should learn to mount from the ground, so here goes:

- To mount, stand on the left side of your horse and turn your back towards his head. Your left hand reaches across the withers for the right rein, which you hold between your middle and ring fingers. The left rein runs through the palm of your hand. From the beginning, develop the habit of having slight contact with the horse's mouth. This rein contact is a signal to the horse to remain standing in place.

- Next, reach with your left hand, still holding the reins, for the horse's mane in front of the saddle; this will prevent you from pulling on the reins while mounting. With your right hand, turn the stirrup clockwise so the iron is at a right angle to the horse (clockwise, because the leather will then lie flat against your lower leg; if you step into the stirrup from the wrong side, the strap will be twisted like a corkscrew and will give you black-and-blue marks on the inside of your lower leg).

- Place your left foot in the stirrup so that the ball of the foot rests on the iron. Rest your knee against the saddle and reach with your right hand for the cantle. With a good bounce, spring off the ground, lifting your right leg up and over the horse's croup, with your upper body leaning slightly forward. While in motion, turn your body towards the horse's head without letting the tip of your boot hit his rib cage. You should have enough spring so that your right foot does not hit the horse's croup, but not so much that you land heavily in the saddle.

- As you sink gently into the saddle, feel with your toe for the right stirrup. Slip your foot in, making sure the ball of your foot is securely centered in the iron. Gather your reins and give the horse a few encouraging and grateful pats on the neck.

DISMOUNTING

To dismount, place both reins in your left hand and support yourself with your right hand on the pommel of the saddle.

- Kick your foot out of the right stirrup, lift yourself up out of the saddle and swing your right leg across the croup of the horse.
- Now reach for the cantle with your right hand and the mane with your left hand. Once balanced, slide elegantly down to the ground.

Vaulting Out of the Saddle

More athletic types can try vaulting off the horse.

- With someone holding the horse's head, let go of the reins, hold on to the pommel with both hands and kick both feet out of the stirrups.
- Gather momentum with your legs by swinging them forward. Quickly swing back and over the horse's croup, twist your body away from the horse and hit the ground with both feet simultaneously.

with which you can apply proper aids.

The lower legs are held comfortably and with light contact alongside the horse's body at or slightly behind the girth.

The knees are bent at a slight angle, with a light contact between knee and saddle.

The thighs are slightly turned inward. The proper position automatically follows from sitting correctly with your seat in the saddle.

JUST SITTING?

Books dealing with the subject of "sitting on a horse" could fill a library. There are many theories and many approaches. As far as we and *this* book are concerned, you start from the bottom up.

PROPER SEAT

The feet belong in the stirrups, with the balls of the feet resting on the iron. The heel is the lowest point because a low heel allows you to have a long leg, and a long leg stabilizes your seat. Try pulling your legs up and you'll quickly realize how unstable you become, particularly when the horse is moving at speed. Another reason is that your legs drive the horse; when your heel is not low enough, the muscles are not properly engaged and there will be nothing

Your seat should first be relaxed, carrying your weight equally on both hips and the inside of your thigh muscles. You are sitting properly when you can feel both seat bones. Don't hunch over, but hold your upper body upright with head held high and shoulders lowered and relaxed.

Always Remain *Relaxed!*

As you look at these photos of expert riders demonstrating what we're talking about, don't just try to copy them in order to avoid making mistakes. You'll only tense up. The goal, during the first weeks of riding, is simply to avoid developing bad habits. Don't worry if your lower legs flop about, your heels come up or your knees leave the saddle. As long as you remain relatively relaxed and keep your seat in the saddle, you'll have a sense of the basics. Everything else will come in time and with practice.

GATHERING THE REINS

Beginning riders usually ride horses in only a snaffle bit, far less complicated that the double reins of a curb and snaffle. The two drawings on the right explain how to hold the reins properly.

- The reins are kept straight and equal in length, held in each hand with the leather running through the little and ring finger and leaving above the index finger.

- The thumb is placed on top of the rein to keep it from slipping. The remainder of the rein simply falls in a loop to the neck of the horse.

- Wrists remain flexible without letting the hands "collapse."

- Arms are slightly bent and held at waist height, always flexible enough for forward and backward movement.

Reins held correctly

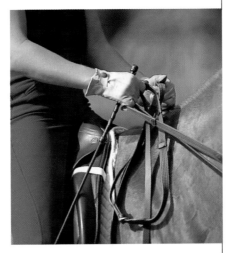

READY TO MOVE...

Finally, you're moving towards the *track*, the path along the wall in an indoor arena or along the fence of an outdoor arena. Since you could turn either to the right or left, your instructor will call out, "Tracking to the right" or "...left," as the case may be. For the first few minutes you'll ride at a walk with long reins. This gives you and your horse the chance to stretch and warm up before serious work begins.

BRACING THE BACK

A horse will step forward at the proper signal. That signal is "bracing" your back, a term used in riding that beginners find hard to understand. And, in reality, from the point of view of anatomy, the back cannot be "braced." Actually, a better command might be: "Shift your weight to your seat bones," since what you do to "brace your back" is push your pelvis slightly forward and shift your weight to your seat bones. Your weight now pushes forward and down. You are not rounding or hollowing your back, and you are not reducing the pressure in the saddle.

What you will find out very quickly is that your horse can feel when you are bracing your back even through

Horse and rider in harmony and unison

the thickest saddle. This action is so distinct that a well-ridden horse will react to just this subtle motion and will simply move forward.

There is, however, more to getting a horse to move forward. In addition to bracing your back, you need to increase the pressure of both lower legs at or slightly behind the girth and slightly relax your hands. A horse that has not become dulled to all aids should move forward. The moment he does this to your satisfaction, immediately reward his obedience by releasing all pressure of your seat and lower legs.

A PRACTICAL TIP

Tightening the Girth and Adjusting Stirrups
After a few minutes of riding, you often have to tighten the girth again. You can tell if that's necessary by reaching down and inserting your hand under the girth (or your instructor will notice that the girth needs to be tightened). Here's how to do it "from above."

Hold both reins in your right hand. Move your left leg forward and lift the saddle flap with your left hand. Also with your left hand, reach for the end of one of the girth straps and tighten it one or two holes. Tighten one strap at a time, because if you loosen both at the same time there is a good chance that the saddle, and you with it, will be on the ground. You don't need to stop in order to tighten your girth. It can be done while the horse is walking.

You can also readjust your stirrups if you find they are either too short or too long (when in doubt, ask your instructor). When adjusting the stirrup leather, the reins are held in one hand. Keep your foot in the stirrup and move your leg back a bit to reach the buckle more easily. Repeat the procedure on the other side if need be, moving the buckle the same number of holes, because having uneven stirrups means you won't be able to sit straight in the saddle.

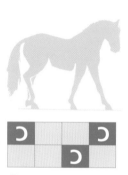

Three legs on the ground

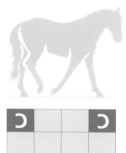

Lateral pair on the ground

Three legs on the ground

Diagonal pair on the ground

Footfall sequence at walk

THE WALK

Beginners find that the walk is the most comfortable gait. It's a slow and regular four-beat, quiet motion without a suspension phase, and will not bounce you around on your horse's back.

The Tempo

The drawing above shows the sequence of the horse's legs at the walk. Walking takes place in three different rhythms, determined by the length of stride and frequency of footfalls: a *medium walk* is the gait you will work in most of the time (it's also known as the *working tempo*); the *extended walk* is a longer gait used for more difficult exercises; and the *collected walk* is a compact gait used in dressage.

Giving with the Reins and Activating Your Legs

Don't consider the walk simply as a welcome opportunity to rest. For your horse to walk properly requires effort on your part. For one thing, you must follow with your hands so as not to interfere with the motion of your horse's head. For another, you should always actively drive with your legs so your horse does not fall asleep under you. Therefore, you alternate between tensing the muscles in your lower legs: first your right, then your left...repeating with each stride of your horse. This action on your part will keep a well-trained horse at a brisk walk. If not, brace your back and use your seat, always in rhythm with the horse's motion.

Aids for moving off from the halt or walk

Explanation of symbols:

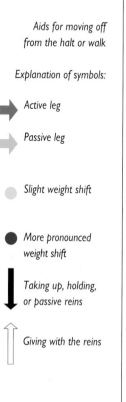

Active leg

Passive leg

Slight weight shift

More pronounced weight shift

Taking up, holding, or passive reins

Giving with the reins

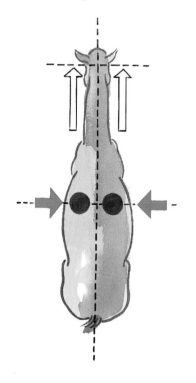

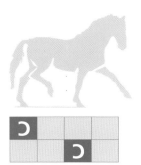

Diagonal pair on the ground
(right forefoot and left hind foot)

Suspension phase

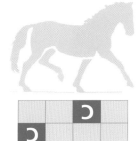

Diagonal pair on the ground
(left forefoot and right hind foot)

Suspension phase

THE TROT

The trot is a lively two-beat gait. It has four different tempi: *working trot, medium trot, extended trot,* and *collected trot.* The moment of suspension between each beat is when the rider is likely to bounce. While an experienced horseback rider can absorb this vertical push with his pelvis, the beginner usually is subjected to what physicists call "inertia of mass." The novice rises and then falls back hard into the saddle when the horse's hooves strike the ground.

Asking for a Trot

To get your horse to move into a trot, use the same aids as when you ask your horse to walk, but more firmly. If the horse is already at the walk, it's easier to increase the tempo and you'll therefore be able to do it with less effort. However, to move from a halt into a trot, your aids need to be more active and will involve more pressure.

As a beginner, you will usually go into the trot from a walk. You do this the same way as if you were asking your horse to move off in a walk: let your weight sink forward and down into the saddle, add pressure with your lower legs at or slightly behind the girth while at the same time you "give" with your hands.

The footfall of the trot is shown above, but we will not discuss what it feels like. Instead we will tell you how you and your horse can make life easier for both of you by a technique known as posting.

Footfall sequence at trot

Aids for moving off

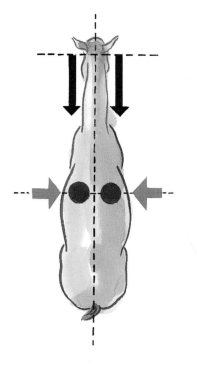

83

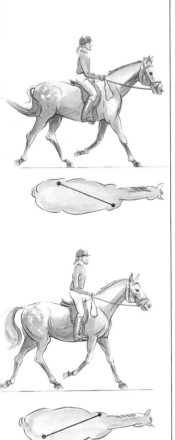

Posting the Trot

Posting is simply rising out of the saddle when a diagonal pair of legs pushes off the ground, then sinking back down when the opposite pair pushes off. Then you rise again, sink again, and so on. But how do you know which pair of legs pushing off the ground tells you when you are supposed to rise?

The secret, at least for novices, is to look: your horse's outside hind leg will signal when you should rise. Although you can't see that leg, you can watch your horse's shoulder. Since the trot has a diagonal footfall, the outside hind leg and the inside front leg move forward at the same time. Therefore, the forward movement of the inside shoulder is the signal to rise.

The Less Effort the Better

Try not to lift yourself too far out of the saddle. The closer you are to the saddle, the less distance you have to sink back into the saddle. In other words, the less effort you spend, the more comfortable it will be for you and for the horse. Let the horse's impulsion help you rise, then sink back as if you are controlling the way you bounce.

The "hinge" that makes posting possible is your knees, which means your knees must keep in close contact with the saddle. Since the impulse for rising out of the saddle comes from your ankles, the position of the lower legs does not change. As you flex the muscles of the lower legs, you gain an added benefit by making sure the horse steps out lively.

Changing Diagonals

Constantly posting on the same diagonal is a burden for the horse. It's therefore recommended that you change diagonals whenever you change directions. Your riding instructor will most likely require this of you, and he or she will remind you when to do so. Changing diagonals is easy: you just sit out one stride by bouncing once, then you simply continue posting as you did before.

Posting on the correct diagonal: rising out of the saddle when the outside hind leg touches the ground and the inside shoulder moves forward, then sinking back when the inside hind leg touches the ground and the outside shoulder moves forward.

Sitting Trot

You have already practiced sitting out one stride when changing diagonals when posting. Now we will torture you a bit: that's what a sitting trot will feel like. In the beginning, the horse's motion in a sitting trot will shake you up quite badly.

Your horse will also be quite uncomfortable if you bounce around like a sack of potatoes. To find out what it's like for the horse, strap on a backpack, leaving the straps longer than they should be, and start running. Your shoulder and back muscles will automatically tense up to counteract the constant punishment you're inflicting on your back. That's what the horse does, and it increases the problem. Your seat hits the saddle even harder, and there is very little chance of learning how to sit to a trot.

Remain Relaxed

We have two suggestions: 1) don't pinch your seat muscles together and 2) try to keep as relaxed as possible, no matter how uncomfortable. Learning to sit to a trot will happen only through practice, by staying relaxed and having the courage to tolerate some discomfort. Improvement will automatically come when you accommodate the motion of the horse beneath you. At that moment, you'll notice that your pelvis tips slightly forward when the horse raises his back. That is what you want to happen: you want to move in sync with the horse's movement. As soon as the horse's back comes down again, your pelvis moves with it back to its original position. As soon as this happens, you'll have discovered the secret of how to sit at a trot. And you will be on this side of comfort for the rest of your riding life.

Both Legs Remain Active

You use your lower legs positioned at the girth with each stride of the sitting trot or every second stride of the posting trot to keep the horse's momentum going. And, if you have already successfully conquered this skill, you will be able to brace your back naturally.

Heike is demonstrating a posting trot without raising herself too high out of the saddle.

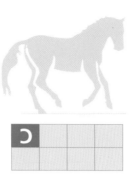

Footfall sequence at canter

One leg on the ground

Three legs on the ground

Diagonal pair of legs on the ground

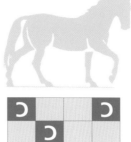

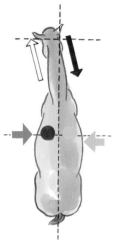

Aids for striking off into a canter on the left lead

CANTER

The canter is an animated three-beat gait during which the rider is tossed around less than at the trot. We distinguish between a *left lead* and a *right lead* canter, depending on whether the left or the right legs reach further forward. The sequence of canter footfall is shown in the series of drawings above.

The Light Seat

Cantering can be done either with a "light" (called "half-seat" or "two-point") or "close contact" (or "three-point") seat. Cantering with a light seat is even easier than trotting. You simply rise out of the saddle by supporting yourself with your knees against the saddle and by placing weight in your heels. Bend forward at the waist ever so slightly and rest your hands on either side of the horse's neck. The light seat, which allows the horse to move unhindered, is usually used in the open and on the trail.

Riding Close Contact and Aids

Cantering in close contact requires a little bit more work. A horse that is being asked to canter has to be slightly flexed, or bent, because the horse must reach further out either with his left or right pair of legs. Since we will tell you more about *flexing* and *position* in the next chapter, for now let us point out only that you position your horse to the inside by shortening the inside rein to the degree that you want the horse to flex. Your inside lower leg is at the girth. Increasing the pressure

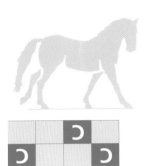

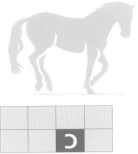

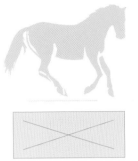

Three legs on the ground

One leg on the ground
(right forefoot)

Suspension phase

of this leg drives the horse into the canter. Your outside leg remains passive, resting about the width of a hand behind the girth.

Positioning the legs in such a way automatically moves your hips into the proper position, with the side hip slightly forward and the weight shifted to the inside seat bone. That gives enough room for the horse's inside shoulder to reach forward. When the

horse strikes off into the canter, your inside active leg maintains the tempo. In rhythm with the up-and-down movement of the horse's head, you give lightly with the inside rein to support a free forward movement.

However, American riders should be aware that some horses have been

trained to take the canter from the so-called outside aids: the outside rein turns the horse's head to the outside and the rider's active outside leg behind the girth asks the horse to canter.

Ludger Beerbaum demonstrating the actively driving inside leg.

FROM SLB'S JOURNAL

Fear of Speed

I still vividly remember my first riding lesson. The last person on line, I was more or less hanging in the saddle with a very docile (if not "lazy") horse underneath me. When the command came for the first time "Get ready for canter," my dear little horse obviously thought that this was nothing that either one of us wanted to do. Accordingly, he proceeded to go in a straight line to the center of the riding ring and place his head very comfortably on the instructor's shoulder.

I simply sat there, watching what the rest of the group was doing as they cantered. And how glad I was to have found a quiet spot in the middle of the ring. It looked pretty wild to me and I have never been a hero.

But at the next lesson the instructor thought it was time for me to try cantering, promising me in his best Swabian dialect: "Sibylle, this will be so much fun." Trusting in him, I stayed with the group. My horse galloped off, taking me along on this wonderful ride. It was indeed beautiful.

Believe me, a canter is really special. Compared to the trot, it is easy to sit to. During the early stage of my riding education, it was the best indication of what the sport was all about. To this day I think with a smile about my first canter; for the first time I was truly happy in the saddle.

LEFT, RIGHT— THE TECHNIQUES OF RIDING

Always riding in a straight line is not only boring, it limits what horses can do. They can do everything that a car can do: stop (and faster), turn left, turn right, go forward and backward. In addition, they can do something that an automobile cannot: they can move sideways and at different speeds. If that is not enough, horses can turn in a tight circle, something that drivers with only the smallest of cars can even dream about. However, horses can do all this only if given proper instructions, which involves a bit more than simply turning a steering wheel.

BASIC TRAINING

STOP, PLEASE!

Stopping a horse involves more than just pulling on the reins. Aside from the fact that pulling is painful for the horse, we can stop much more elegantly, using halts. We have two different versions: the half-halt and the halt.

The Half-Halt

The half-halt is used constantly. No matter what you want to do—go faster or slower, turn or move laterally, back up or prepare for a jump—the command always begins with a half-halt. It is the aid that prepares the horse for additional instructions to come and, for a well-trained horse, it is the signal to "pay attention, something else will happen."

The Signal

Your horse is moving at a walk. You are sitting on both of your seat bones. You have a light and even contact with the reins, which encourages the horse to carry his head slightly in front of the vertical. Your hands follow the animal's forward movement by giving with the reins at each movement of his head. To give the half-halt signal, restrain the horse's head by squeezing with your outside hand. At the same time, apply the active pressure of your lower leg and lower back. That is all you have to do.

Always use the outside rein regardless of whether you are riding in an indoor or outdoor arena. Out on the trail, however, you may freely choose which rein you want to hold. But remember to alternate between sides often to keep the horse from becoming one-sided.

The first phase of the half-halt is where you "hold" the outside rein. For the "halt" (see drawing) you hold both reins.

In the second phase you "give" with the rein but without losing contact with the horse's mouth.

Half-Halts

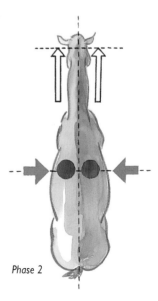

Phase 1   Phase 2

A Matter of Feeling

How these half-halts influence your horse depends on how well trained he is and the degree of emphasis with which you apply your aids. If they are applied gently, a well-trained horse will turn his ears towards you to find out what the next command is. However, if you repeat the aid with a bit more force, he will slow down. Increasing the strength with which you apply the aid will encourage the horse to shift into the next "lower gear." How much emphasis to add varies; it's a matter of feeling.

Each horse reacts differently. Some horses are so sensitive, they barely need a hint. However, those are horses you will probably meet much later in your riding career, privately owned animals that require a rider with a developed and independent seat. Others, the ones you will come in contact with when first taking lessons, need a more forceful message. (School horses tend to become dull due to the many uncoordinated movements of countless generations of beginners.) You simply need to experiment. With enough practice, you'll figure out the necessary amount of effort that specific horses need.

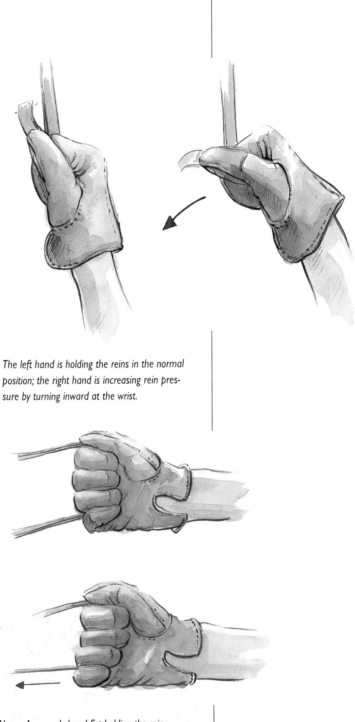

The left hand is holding the reins in the normal position; the right hand is increasing rein pressure by turning inward at the wrist.

Above: A normal closed fist holding the rein

Below: "Giving" the reins by opening up the little finger

The Halt

The signal to the horse to stop is preceded by a half-halt. If the half-halt is given properly, the horse will wait for the next command, which is given by pushing yourself deeper into the saddle. Start by bracing your lower back and either maintaining a steady pressure on the reins or gently pulling them back a few inches while actively driving with your lower legs. If you have used the proper amount of "drive and hold" coordination, the horse will halt and stand.

Braking with the Hindquarters

You may find it curious that you drive a horse forward while you want him to stop, something that has already happened when you practiced half-halts. Forget the logic that applies to driving a car and instead imagine how your actively driving lower legs prompt the horse's hindquarters. He will step further under his center of gravity. While the horse would normally move forward from the impulse created by the pressure of your legs, your restraining with the reins prevents it. The horse reacts to your signal and does not simply roll forward to a halt, as inertia would dictate. Instead, he begins "braking" with his hindquarters and comes to a square, balanced and controlled halt.

Pressure Creates Counter-Pressure

Here, too, you must find the proper "dosage" through constant practice and with different horses. But even if you are dealing with a particularly clumsy horse that reacts to all your efforts with ignorance, don't pull on the reins and don't press deeply into the saddle. Pressure creates counter-pressure, and horses have a very efficient method to avoid doing what they don't want to do: they grab hold of the bit, stiffen their back and neck, and throw a body mass of more than one-half of a ton against your arm muscles.

If your first attempt at a balanced halt is unsuccessful, don't give up and don't give in. If necessary, repeat the aids several times, increasing the degree of intensity so that your horse does not have a chance to lean on the bit.

"Braking" with the hindquarters: Heike is activating both lower legs and bracing her back to signal "halt."

The Perfect Halt

There is more to the exercise even when your horse has reacted properly and has come to a halt. After he has halted, he should stand squarely with his weight equally divided on all four legs and hold his head so his face is vertical to the ground. That is the perfect halt.

If, instead, your horse is standing quite well in front but not with his hindquarters, use your lower leg to drive him. Use the leg on the side where you want his hind leg to step further under his body. A well-trained horse will willingly move that leg into the proper position.

Your seat will tell you whether a horse's hindquarters are squarely under him. When both hind legs are properly positioned, both of your seat bones will be comfortable and evenly placed in the saddle. But if one hind leg is not quite there, your seat will be lower on that side. With time you'll acquire the feeling. And here, too, practice makes perfect.

Above: This is not quite right. The horse is not standing square and his head is too far in front of the vertical.

Below: This is what a square and balanced halt should look like.

Going Left and Right— or How to "Wrap" a Horse Around Your Lower Leg

The easiest of all the turning possibilities for a horse is called the *turn in motion*, where you only have to flex your horse around your lower leg.

This concept may test your imagination. How are you supposed to flex 1200 pounds of animal around your leg by simple pressure? But it is possible because the horse under you has, we would hope, learned in his basic training to react to a driving lower leg. The horse has also been taught to react to a shift of the rider's weight and to the reins that signal a change in direction.

Here we have reached a very important point that needs special emphasis: *a turn in motion is not initiated with your hands.*

Changing Directions

Imagine your horse is going in a straight line. You are driving with both legs equally and the reins are in light but equal contact. You want to change direction—for instance, go to the left. To begin with, and as always, you alert your horse to the fact that you are asking him to do something by asking for a half-halt. As the horse now waits for what is coming next, you shift your weight perceptibly to your left seat bone, turn your left shoulder (and thereby your whole body) to the left and increase the amount of "drive" pressure with your left leg at the girth. At the same time, you take up the left

rein lightly, not pulling the horse's head into the new direction but only shortening the rein to show him the direction. You also give ever so lightly with the right rein, just enough so your horse is able to bend to the left. Now the horse can flex around your left leg and thereby turn to the left.

What You Need to Think About

For this exercise, you have to think of several things at once:

- Don't collapse your hip, because it would have the exact opposite effect: rather than shifting your weight in this case to the left, you would shift it to the outside.
- Your back remains straight and your left shoulder is turned slightly in the desired direction.
- Don't "throw away" the outside rein. This rein limits the amount of bend and allows the horse to lean against your leg, giving him stability. The outside rein prevents his drifting in the wrong direction.
- Your outer leg (here, the right leg) remains in contact with the horse. The leg is held slightly behind the girth. It doesn't drive but simply maintains contact to prevent the horse's outside hindquarters from drifting out (here, to the right). The horse is also supposed to properly flex his back. What we *don't* want is: "first the shoulder turns the corner, then the rest somehow drags behind." The *entire* horse must flex, and your outside leg acts as the block for the hip. Remember, you are to "wrap" the horse around your inside leg.

More on Turns

A right-hand turn is done in the same way except by using the opposite aids. Turns are first practiced at a walk and later the trot and canter (the faster gaits will be easier because of their momentum).

Whether you are doing half-halts, halts or changing direction, you should always be in close contact with the saddle. Only when you have gained some experience should you change direction while posting or when cantering in a two-point seat.

On the left, horse and rider are in harmony. On the right, the collapsed hip is counter-productive.

LATERAL MOVEMENTS (OR LEG-YIELDING)

This is the moment when any riding instructor reading this book raises an eyebrow and says: "Leg yielding at this stage of the game? You must be kidding!"

Let us quickly explain that we have no intention of asking for *traverse* or *renverse* or any other sophisticated high-school movement. But everybody has to start leg-yielding exercises sometime, and after all they do tell us a great deal about the effectiveness and correctness of the aids we have been using. Even if your instructor never asks you to do these exercises, it never hurts to know them and practice them on your own.

Basic Leg-Yielding

In leg-yielding, as the horse moves forward his inside legs cross over the outside legs. His front legs are on the outside track and the hind legs are on the inside track.

Your first attempts at this movement should take place in an arena, either indoors or outdoors, since a wall or fence is helpful for the beginner to orient himself. It's best to start at a corner and move along the long side of the arena counterclockwise on the left rein. Get the horse to yield to your right leg. Now you do a half-halt, sit deeper in the saddle, halt and then drive on.

Bend the horse to the right, away from the direction of movement, and slightly increase the right rein contact. Shift your weight to your right seat bone to drive the horse forward. Your right lower leg is driving slightly behind the girth. Your left lower leg, slightly behind the girth, maintains contact to hold the tempo. If you have managed neither to lose your stirrups nor raise your heels, you have proba-

To carry out proper lateral movements, you have to pay special attention that your hip does not collapse.

bly achieved a skill usually reserved for more experienced riders.

You may carry a long dressage whip in your right hand to use to reinforce your driving leg, although sometimes just the fact that it's there is all a horse needs to see. Lay the whip across your right thigh, pointing in the direction of the horse's croup, when it's not in use.

Position and Flexion

If your horse has properly learned the basics, it should be possible for you to do this exercise. Use your right leg to drive your horse forward. He should begin to move sideways and cross his front and hind legs at the same time. He should remain straight, not bent in the neck (which can be corrected with the outer rein). His hind legs should not veer in the opposite direction, which you accomplish by holding him with your lower left leg behind the girth. Do not let your hips collapse.

To move the horse laterally in the other direction, you simply do everything in mirror image. A horse can also be turned to the center of the arena with leg yields. That, however, will be a bit more difficult in the beginning, because you don't have a wall or fence as a perimeter and your horse can escape your aids more easily.

At this stage in your riding career, your instructor will probably choose to test you with the following or similar question: When you ride on the left rein and the horse is bent toward the center of the ring, which of your legs does he yield to? The answer is, of course, your left.

Where Is "Inside" and Where Is "Outside"?

Direction is not a matter of left or right but only of *inside* and *outside*. "Inside" is always the side to which the horse is bent or flexed. Normally it's in the direction of the center of the ring, but there are times when you will ride movements on tracks and serpentines (explained in detail later) where the original position changes. If, logically speaking, the *inside* is the concave side of the horse, it stands to reason that the convex side is the *outside*, regardless of which side is the leading side or whether you are in an indoor arena or outside in the open.

The Active Leg Is Always the Inside Leg

With regard to the term *active leg*, a horse always yields to the inside leg. In other words, the rider's leg determines the direction in which the horse is flexed. If he is flexed to the left, it stands to reason the active leg will be the left leg, which urges the horse to move forward laterally and outside to the right. Conversely, a horse that is flexed to the right reacts to the right leg and moves left. All clear?

Advanced Leg-Yielding

Many other lateral movements are developed from the action of an active leg, including the *shoulder-in*, *traverse*, *renverse* and *traversal*. Lateral movements are excellent means of training the horse and rider. However, these exercises are for the advanced rider and are mentioned here only for the sake of completeness.

Advanced lateral movements
Above: Shoulder-in
Below: Traversal

TURNING

Here is another opportunity to demonstrate that you are by now capable of "wrapping" your horse around your leg.

Turn on the Forehand

As the name suggests, a turn on the forehand moves the horse 180 degrees around his front legs. The front hooves step in place while the hindquarters move in a half circle around them. The exercise is always done from the halt.

It's best to practice along the long side of the arena and counterclockwise on the left rein. To avoid your horse's hitting his nose against the wall, you position him on a track away from the wall.

Your instructor will ask for a turn on the forehand to the right because the horse's head is flexed to that side. You drive with your inside leg behind the girth and hold with your outside lower leg, which is placed a good hand-width behind the girth. The horse should now take the first step around his forehand. If he hesitates, correct your seat and the position of the horse and then try again. Aim for one step at a time. This exercise should give you a sense for position and flexion, and it's most effective when you take your time.

Turn on the Hindquarters (Haunches)

While turning on the forehand is relatively easy, it is much more difficult turning a horse on the hindquarters (also known as a turn on the haunches).

Although this is a more advanced movement, you should know how it works.

You start by squarely halting your horse parallel to the wall or fence of the riding ring. The command is: "Turning on the hindquarters to the left." This means that the horse is flexed to the left and the front legs will step in a half circle (180 degrees) around the hind legs.

To initiate the turn, you shift your weight to the inside seat bone (the left one for a turn to the left) and place your inside lower leg on the girth. The inside rein gives slightly without losing contact while the outside rein remains in place. The outside leg behind the girth drives the horse's forelegs around his haunches. The inside leg controls each step, making sure that the horse walks forward and not back.

The first three steps tend to be the easiest because the horse has little problem moving around his inside hindquarters.

However, from that point forward the horse tends to move his inside hindquarters too. Small leg movements are acceptable, but too many are frowned upon. That's why you should allow your horse to complete each step, then reposition yourself well in the saddle, and only then let him take another step until he has reversed his direction.

Do not overdo either type of turn. These exercises are demanding both for you and your horse. Take your time. Be satisfied with half a turn to start with, and give your horse lots of praise when you and he are finished.

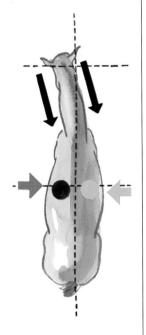

Aids used for "turning on the forehand"

Sharp Turns

Once you have advanced to this level of riding, a turn on the hindquarters can also be done at a walk and trot. If you do it from a trot, you first change gaits down to a walk, and—without stopping—smoothly start the turn. At the completion—again without stopping—take one step at the walk and go into the trot.

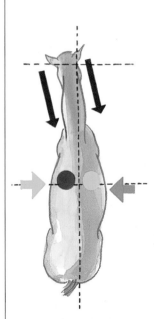

Aids for a turn on the hindquarters (haunches)

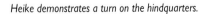

Heike demonstrates a turn on the hindquarters.

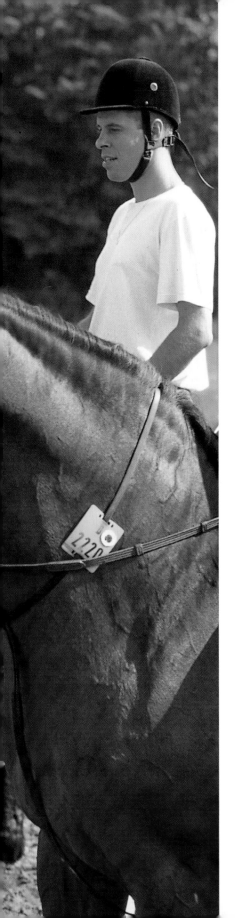

RIDING
IN THE ARENA

Few riders want to spend all their lives riding indoors. You long for the moment when you can mount your horse and be out on the trail, unhindered by walls or fences. However, work in the riding arena is essential. That's where you can build up your horse's stamina with exercises that enable him to carry you without undue wear and tear. In addition, arena riding teaches you good manners, which are much more than simple etiquette. Born out of experience, they serve to keep horses and riders safe, a fact you'll appreciate as soon as you encounter a busy ring.

ETIQUETTE IN THE RIDING RING

"Is the Gate Clear?"

The very first rule to remember is never to enter an indoor or outdoor riding arena, whether on a horse or leading one, without having clearly announced your intention. The standard way is to call out "Rider entering"—a polite request to those in the arena to make room. As soon as no one is near the gate, any person who has a good view of the arena will call out "Gate is clear." That response is the green light to enter.

Mounting and Dismounting in the Center

Mounting, tightening your girth and dismounting should be done without getting in anybody else's way. The center of the arena is usually the best place for getting on, unless there is a mounting block in one of the corners.

Proper Distance

Keep a safe distance from other riders. Even if you are in the ring with your best friend and have the absolute perfect four-legged buddy under your saddle, keep at least three strides (approximately the length of a horse) between you and any other rider. Even the most peace-loving horse can become frightened and start kicking.

The "Miss Manners" of riding suggests that you don't interfere with anybody else riding in the same arena.

The Track

The term "riding on track" is often used. The track is the "road" along the perimeter of the arena on which the horses move. It is easy to recognize in a less well-cared for arena because the path that horses have traveled is seldom level (for the sake of horses' legs, leveling should be done regularly).

It's not difficult to imagine what would happen if every rider in the arena would pick his or her own path. For that reason, the rules of most arenas state that students practicing on their own must do so along the wall of an indoor arena or the fence of an outdoor arena.

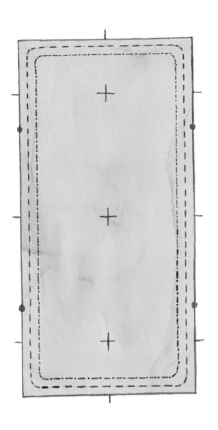

- - - *Outside track*

- · - ·· *Inside track*

Rules of Traffic
The following rules of traffic have been established for arena riding, although they may vary from stable to stable:

• The Outside Track Belongs to the "Swift"
Riders who move at the faster gaits stay on the outside track. Riders who either trot or walk their horses are expected to make room for those who are cantering by moving to the inside track. For safety reasons, the distance between each horse should be at least the length of two horses. A rider who is cantering passes on the outside track. Since getting out of the way may not be done quickly enough, start out on the inside track if you intend only to walk your horse.

Another requirement for riding in many indoor arenas is that the whip is held in the inside hand.

• Track Before Circle
Riders on the outside track have right of way over those who are making a circle. If you ride a circle, you pass inside any riders who are on the outside track.

• Left Hand Has "Right of Way"
When several riders are working their horses in different parts of the arena, those moving on the left lead have the right of way on the outside track over those moving in the opposite direction on the right lead.

At many stables, the rule is to pass "left hand to left hand." This means that riders pass by keeping to the right.

• Outside Trackers Remain
Sometimes, during a group lesson, riders ride in different directions. If the instructor orders that riders change direction, those who are already on the outside track remain there.

SCHOOL FIGURES

Horses are creatures of habit. When you are working alone and practicing your school figures in the arena, we feel you should always follow the same sequence that will be required in a dressage test.

LETTERS MARK THE SPOT

The person or persons responsible for the letter designation used to mark the dressage arena is unknown, and a good thing, too, because they certainly have annoyed generations of horseback riders. The only thing that can be said about this system of lettering is that there isn't one. Those who want to memorize the arrangement of letters may want to use the following mnemonic device that somebody came up with:

> **A**ll **K**ids **E**at **H**oney
> **C**hildren **M**ust **B**e **F**ed

Working in a normal arena is a little easier because symbols—called points—have been added which, at least some of the time, do follow a system. These symbols are points of orientation, guiding the rider on the proper path:

HB points, often added to the letters in the middle on both of the long sides of the arena, mark half the arena, or "Halbe Bahn" in German. In the "dressage squares" you will find the letters E and B at these points.

Transition Points: There are four, two at the beginning and two at the end of each long side of the arena. The corresponding letters are K, H, M and F.

Circle Points: The number of points depends on the size of the arena. A 40m by 20m arena accommodates two circles indicated by six points. One is on each short side in the center: A and C; two are on each long side farther in than the transition points—shown at left as four dark circles. The circles also have center points: D and G. But the points are not posted since it's impossible to post letters in the middle of the arena.

An arena measuring 20m by 60m accommodates three circles. In addition to the two mentioned above,

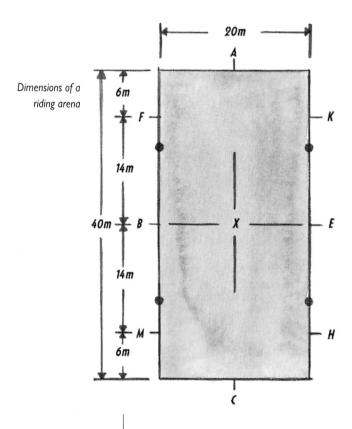

Dimensions of a riding arena

another circle can be ridden in the center of the arena. Often there are balls suspended from the ceiling that outline the dimension of this circle.

The **X** is the center of the dressage square: it is the point where the imaginary lines drawn from A and C and from E to B cross. Unless a ball suspended from the ceiling points to the X, you must use your imagination.

Riding on the Flat

Exercises have the same goal for both horse and rider: *flexing* and *positioning*. Flexing is best practiced by riding serpentine lines, which a good instructor will always include in a lesson. Serpentines not only break up the boredom of always riding along the track, they also serve as suppling and strengthening exercises. A

horse by nature was not meant to carry a rider, which is the reason why certain muscles must be exercised and brought into balance. A horse is not a machine that once "tuned up" will automatically stay in top working order. As with every other athlete, his form must be maintained through constant training.

Flexing and Positioning Improves Coordination

Working with your horse on the serpentine makes him supple, exercises his muscles and improves his coordination. Regular, focused workouts will also be of advantage to you: you will improve and coordinate your aids and communicate better with your horse, all of which will also come in handy when you are out on the trail.

Flexing and positioning:
Left : "Straight"
Middle: "Positioned"
Right : "Flexed"

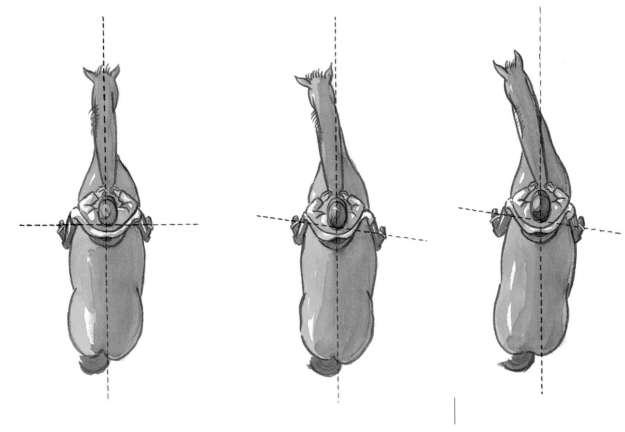

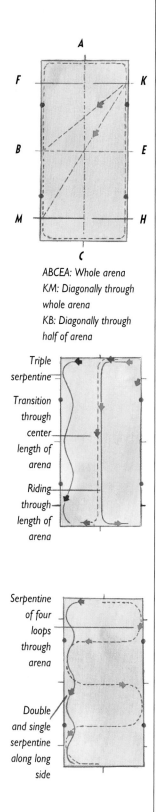

ABCEA: Whole arena
KM: Diagonally through
whole arena
KB: Diagonally through
half of arena

Triple
serpentine

Transition
through
center
length of
arena

Riding
through
length of
arena

Serpentine
of four
loops
through
arena

Double
and single
serpentine
along long
side

Movements

Transition Through Whole Arena

This frequently heard command presents a simple change of direction from one point, diagonally through the arena, to the opposite point. After turning the corner, turn at the point of transition and ride straight on the diagonal to the opposite point. If you use a trot, change diagonals about one horse length before reaching the point of transition. If you canter (which you do only after you are more experienced), do a half-halt at the point of transition, change to a walk and then pick up a canter on the other lead.

Transition Through Half of Arena

Here you start after turning the corner at the point of transition, then go diagonally to the opposite (HB) point. When trotting or cantering, follow the same routine as outlined in "transition through the whole arena" above.

Transition Through Center Length of Arena

Begin at the mid-point on the short side and ride straight through the length of the arena to the opposite short side, where you change leads. This exercise, which is seldom practiced during regular lessons, is required in many dressage tests. Should you ever compete in dressage, remember that the judges are particularly interested in seeing how well you ride your horse absolutely straight through the center of the arena. That means that the hind feet should travel in the same track as the front feet, not in separate tracks. (More about this when we discuss making the horse obedient to the aids).

In riding through the length of the arena, you don't change direction at the second circle point but continue in the same circle and on the same diagonal.

Riding Serpentines

Riding serpentines bends and flexes your horse. The drawing on the left (middle and below) explains what is involved.

A **simple serpentine** along the long wall is ridden so that the distance between the track and the top of the serpentine is approximately 5 meters.

For a **double serpentine** along the long side of the arena, the serpentine curves about 2½ meters away from the track. When riding serpentines, always start and finish at the point of transition.

When riding serpentines through the arena, the first and the last curve of a loop is considered a whole even though you actually only ride one half. If you ride an uneven number of curves, you always end in the same direction you started. When riding an even number, it will be the opposite direction. The more curves you ride, the better your sense of space has to be. Ideally, all curves are of the same size.

Riding serpentines at a posting trot and changing diagonals at every curve is a wonderful exercise. Those who have done it often enough will become so good that they automatically pick up the correct diagonal when on the trail, for which their horses will be immensely grateful. In addition, knowing how to ride serpentines comes in very handy when you have to maneuver around trees and bushes.

Circles

Riding circles is also a wonderful exercise for you and your horse. When riding a circle, you turn at the "circle point" and continue evenly around the circumference through an imaginary X in the center and on to the opposite circle point. Continue on the circle until you are instructed to do otherwise. The object is to ride a perfect circle, not an Easter egg with the kind of flattened corners shown in the diagram.

Another movement is to ride a circle as before, but at the X point in the center of the arena, you change directions and start a second circle. Do not ride a "figure eight," but remain on the second circle until you are told otherwise.

Change Direction Through the Circle

Being asked to change directions in the circle involves riding a serpentine. The transition takes place at the circle point on the long side toward the center of the arena, at which point you ride a half-curve to the center. There, you change directions and continue riding a half-curve to the opposite circle point. Again, stay on the second circle until otherwise instructed.

About-Turn (Volte) and Its Variations

An **about-turn** (also known as a **volte**) is a small circle of about 6–10 meters in diameter. An exercise for advanced riders, it is usually ridden on the long side of the arena. The horse must bend powerfully and your aids must be exact.

At the command "About-turn—go," you turn to the center of the arena and circle your horse back to the track.

At "About-turn reverse—go," you start as above but you don't finish the circle. Instead, you change direction after riding one half of the circle and ride in a straight line back to the track.

The command "Reverse from the corner" (or "...next corner") asks you to ride the above "about-turn reverse" in a corner, always done along the long side of the arena.

A "figure eight" is rarely performed, but it's an excellent exercise for the advanced rider. Here you start riding an "about-turn" and then add a second "about-turn" in the opposite direction.

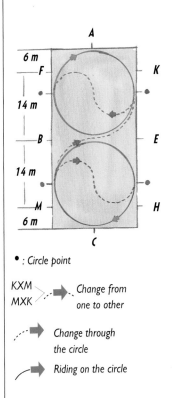

• : Circle point

KXM
MXK   Change from
           one to other

           Change through
           the circle

           Riding on the circle

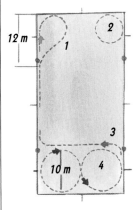

1: From the corner—
about-turn
2: About-turn
3: Left turn on the track
4: Figure eight

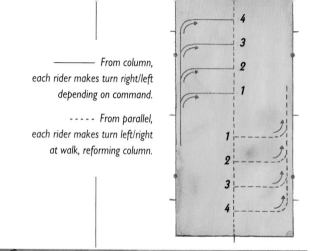

———— From column, each rider makes turn right/left depending on command.

- - - - - From parallel, each rider makes turn left/right at walk, reforming column.

Lining Up and End-of-Class

At the start of each group lesson at many stables, students line up in the center of the arena facing the instructor. One rider, who has been chosen by the instructor, will lead the group and walk off first when instructed, with the rest of the class following behind. All this is done in a very relaxed fashion.

Similarly, group lessons often finish in what is called a "formation." Students have been riding during the lesson in a column. When the instructor announces the end of the lesson, the leader turns and walks in a straight line to the center of the ring. The next rider follows one-horse length behind the leader, followed by the next rider and the next—and so on—until the group is lined up in a perfect row. This fun conclusion to a lesson is usually done at a walk, but it can also be done at a trot.

A PRACTICAL TIP

SLB's Observations of Arena Drill Exercises

"Drill exercises" in any form never appealed to me. I believe that most of them are dull and boring for both people and horses. But to be truthful, many of the drills I have suffered through in the arena have turned out to be worthwhile.

I learned to ride correct school figures and switch diagonals during the posting trot without even thinking. I sit out one stride, post again and continue on my way. It was drilled into me again and again and again until it became second nature.

Not long ago I had reason to be very grateful to my former instructor for drilling me the way he did. The occasion was a trail ride. A heavy rain had soaked me to the bones, I was dead tired and had several more miles to go before reaching the stable. I still functioned almost automatically, only because of what I had learned during those drill exercises.

It's worth remembering that whatever you are taught during those early stages of your horseback riding life will become a gift to all the horses you ride in the future.

OBEDIENCE TO THE AIDS

To be effective, a horse must be alert, eager, straight, rhythmical and more or less collected. The horse must also obey the aids for any exercise to be carried out properly.

When a Horse "Falls Apart"

When you see a horse looking bored, walking haphazardly or otherwise without coordination, you have a poorly ridden horse that does not obey the aids. His neck and back look stiff, and sometime he hollows his back in defense, with his nose poked way out in front.

Lack of proper riding makes it difficult for a horse to walk straight. His forehand and hindquarters don't move in a straight line. The horse moves heavily, his hindquarters don't step under his body, and he leans on the bit. It's hard work to ride such a horse. The rider is unable to sit properly and the aids are rarely effective. In riding circles, this animal is referred to as a horse that has "fallen apart."

All of the above might be tolerated if it were hard only on the rider. But it's also a problem for the horse because he will be tense, develop the wrong muscles, and put too much weight on his forehand, all of which will, over time, lead to wear and tear. A horse suffering from physical discomfort is less able and willing to obey his rider's aids. Tension starts to mount, and a vicious cycle is in the making.

Above: This is a horse that is obedient to the aids.

Below: The head is carried too high, neck and back are giving way, front legs step nervously and hind legs drag behind. Both rider and horse have a long way to go.

rider braces his back and drives with his legs to activate the horse's hindquarters. As we've discussed earlier, the momentum developed from behind isn't simply allowed to move forward and be dissipated but rather, and in the truest sense, it is "reined in." The rider restrains or packages the horse's forward movement, pushing the weight like an accordion from behind forward onto the bit.

That gives the horse several possibilities. He can lean on the bit, which produces great pressure on the mouth. He can pick up his head, which hollows his back and causes the rider's weight to become extremely uncomfortable to him. He can roll his chin to his chest, which tenses his neck muscles.

The horse in the above photo is "rolling" his neck and leaning on the bit; the horse below is pulling above the bridle.

A well-ridden horse looks entirely different. With well-developed muscles he steps under his hindquarters so they can carry the weight; his top line is round and his back is flexible. The horse walks eagerly and is supple and attentive. He carries his nose at or slightly behind the vertical and chews or plays with the bit comfortably (he may even move his lips). The horse is able to carry the rider effortlessly, obedient to the aids. The risk of sustaining physical damage is greatly reduced because the horse walks not just beautifully but according to his natural athletic ability.

How can you bring your horse to move in this way? In the classic English riding style, the leather. It will take many months of practice for you to know whether a horse under you moves any old way or is carrying you with momentum and balance.

The feeling of correctness is very difficult to describe because there are many intermediate phases. As soon as you feel effortlessly balanced in the saddle and carried gently and in synch with the movement of the horse, when the horse does not fight the aids but rather yields because you have done everything right, you have achieved what might be called pure harmony. Only by actually doing it, not studying theory, will you reach this point. Age-old horseback riding wisdom says you learn how to ride by riding.

The only other option for him is to flex his head at the poll, give with his mouth and accept the bit (another expression is *on the bit* or *on the bridle*). That is the response sought by the rider, who immediately rewards the horse by giving with his hands. Now the horse is collected, with supple back muscles. The rider is able to sit, the horse is obedient to the aids and is finally going correctly. But for a horse to do all this, he needs a rider who is able to give his aids correctly as well.

Only by Riding Can You Learn to Ride

This is complicated work. You are asked at any given moment to distinguish between your horse's being stiff or supple, stubborn or willing, tensed up or relaxed. Plus, you are being asked to feel all this through the thickness of saddle

Above: The horse's nose is too far behind the vertical.

Below: The correct walk

WESTERN RIDING

Some of you may be thinking that English riding is so demanding. Isn't there an easier way? Yes, there is. You have probably seen people riding Western style and noticed that their style seems, so much easier and more casual. But going that way, too, requires thorough training, and it can be just as hard as English riding until you reach that relaxed, easy motion you're looking for. True, you may seem to do less work on a Western horse, but you still need solid skills and quick reflexes.

WORKING WITH A PARTNER

While it is difficult to give you detailed instructions about Western riding in one chapter, we can show you the difference between that style and the English style of riding. You can then decide for yourself whether you would like to ride the Western way.

THE WESTERN HORSE

Western horses were developed to be distinctly different from the thoroughbreds and warmbloods that English riders are familiar with, not only from an anatomical standpoint but also in the way they move and interact with riders and tack.

A cowboy who sits in the saddle all day tending his cattle needs to concentrate on his job and not on his horse. Whether the animal's gaits or movements are elegant is irrelevant. Cowboys need to be comfortable and efficient, able to cover long distances without tiring.

The Western horse has to move more or less independently while being immediately obedient to his rider's most subtle aids. This requires a compact build, good carriage, excellent training and conditioning, and above all an innate ability to "think with" the rider. While the number of working cowboys has declined, Western horses are still trained according to these criteria because the advantages are obvious. No matter whether for ranch work, competition or simply

The dreams that Western riding are made of: vacationing at a Spanish guest ranch

a comfortable trail ride, a well-trained Western horse is uncomplicated and relatively easy and safe to handle, which is particularly worthwhile for recreational riders. No wonder Western riding has become very popular throughout the world.

COMPACT, CAPABLE AND SMART

You'll make a very pleasant discovery right from the start, particularly if you are—like one of the authors—of small stature. A Western horse is not as tall as a warmblood or thoroughbred. An average of 15.2 or 15.3 hands is considered tall for American Quarter Horses, Paints and Appaloosas—the predominant breeds used for this type of horsemanship. Many individual horses are even shorter, which makes mounting so much easier. The compact body type is better suited for Western riding than the lively-stepping, long-backed warmbloods and thoroughbreds. That is why many people use Arabs, Morgans and other compactly built breeds for Western riding.

APPAREL

Forget about breeches or jodhpurs if you decide to go Western. Western riders have their clothing preferences, but it has nothing to do with English fashion. Simplicity and practicality is the motto. So, put on your most comfortable jeans (the slim-cut style that keeps your pant legs from bunching or riding up and lets you wear chaps). If

Jean Claude Dysli rides his horse in a quiet canter, called the "lope."

you don't have a pair of cowboy boots, ankle-high paddock or jodhpur boots will do.

Generally speaking, Western riders have always worn "ten gallon" cowboy hats made of felt or straw. Now, however, Western hats with stabilizing inserts that are supposed to increase safety are available. Even though it might be an unpardonable break with the style, there is nothing wrong with wearing a safety helmet, at least until you have developed a secure seat. Some stables will insist on it.

A well-trained Western horse, like this Paint, can be "parked" in the open without any problem.

BRIDLE AND SADDLE

Depending on your riding skill, your horse will be bridled with either a snaffle, a curb or a hackamore or bosal (the last two are bit-less bridles). For the beginner it will be the snaffle bit with a somewhat thinner mouthpiece and larger rings than those generally used for English riding. The reins are split and draped across the horses neck.

The saddle will be Western style with a horn, high cantle and wide fender and skirt. Saddles come in different styles for general or special use, like for cutting or barrel racing. You'll most likely be given an all-purpose model.

Tying the Girth with a Knot

The way to adjust the stirrups and tighten the girth is demonstrated in the photos on the following page. The more old-fashioned way, demonstrated there in the photos on the bottom row, is somewhat more complicated than simply using a buckle.

Adjusting stirrups

The girth on most saddles is tied with a buckle, making tightening easier.

An old-fashioned saddle girth tied with a necktie knot

MOUNTING

Mounting a Western horse need not be the same as the English method, influenced by the military tradition. In Western riding you get the job done as simply as possible.

THE METHOD YOU KNOW

Mounting is easy and efficient.

If you wish, you can mount much the same way you do in the English style. You stand on the left side of the horse with your back to your horse's head. Hold the reins in your left hand. It is essential that the reins are slack, with absolutely no contact with the horse's mouth. Place your left foot in the stirrup and grasp the horn with your left hand and the back of the cantle with your right hand. Then spring off the ground while pulling yourself up and into the saddle.

AN EASIER WAY

The easier way, which you'll see done more often, begins with standing beside the cantle and facing your horse. You hold the reins in your left hand (again, with no contact with the horse's mouth) and you reach for the saddle horn. Place your left foot into the stirrup, reach with your right hand for the cantle and push yourself off the ground, swinging your leg over the croup of the horse and gently lowering yourself in the saddle.

Why should the reins always be slack? After all, what will keep the

horse from walking off while you are mounting? Well, you are dealing with a Western horse who was trained early on not to move until his rider gives a signal. Taking up the reins as you have been taught in English riding would have the opposite effect: the horse would most likely move sideways or back simply trying to escape the pressure.

HANDS OFF, LEGS AWAY

Even before you've taken a single step, you have already learned one of the most important differences between English and Western riding: how you handle the reins. In Western riding, you ride with loose reins because the horse is handled strictly through subtle aids. The rider's legs and back and the reins are used only to change gaits or direction. The Western horse is obedient to the most imperceptible signals and his obedience is immediately rewarded by the rider's no longer applying the aids or pressures.

While a dressage horse is collected through contact with rider's hands, the Western horse walks exclusively on slack reins, maintaining a relaxed self-carriage. The only contact comes from your seat, which gently follows the motion of the horse's gaits.

If this seems a rather shaky proposition, it will take only a few steps until you realize why the Western saddle is considered the "couch" among saddles. You will never have sat on a horse so comfortably and securely. The shape of the saddle's seat puts you accurately in place: the fork and cantle provide support in front and in the back. The wide fenders support your legs and the leather-covered stirrups hold and protect your feet. Even when moving at a fast clip, you'll think that you are sitting in a cradle.

The Western Seat

Your position in a Western saddle is to sit upright, straight and relaxed at the center of gravity. Your weight is placed equally on both seat bones. Your legs hang flexibly and long, without gripping the horse. The tips of your toes are slightly turned in, and your heels are low. Your thighs turn slightly in, but not so much that you are bracing your back. Your elbows belong at your sides and in light contact with your upper body.

The most important aspect of Western riding is to be truly in balance. Remember, you are not driving your horse actively from behind up to the bit at every stride as you do in dressage riding. Instead, you are letting your torso swing passively with the movement of the horse. The horse alone is responsible for maintaining his carriage, the tempo of the gaits and the correct sequence of movements.

As tempting as slouching might be, avoid rounding your back, letting your hips collapse, or sticking your legs and elbows out. This posture looks careless and, worse, it distracts and irritates the horse.

Relaxed at every gait

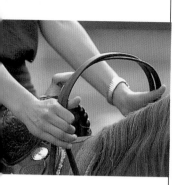

The reins are held in place by forming a bridge.

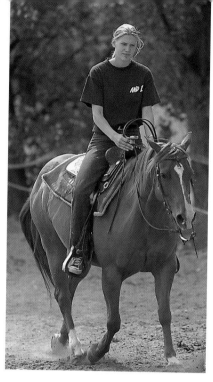

Holding the reins in one hand

Above: Without the use of the index finger

Middle: Index finger separating the reins

Below: Reins held in one hand

It is important that the reins are of equal length and slack enough so that there is no permanent contact with the horse's mouth. If the reins are too short, move your hands apart to separate them. If the reins are too long, shorten them by simply opening your hands slightly so that the ends can slide down. You will now understand why Western reins are relatively heavy: the weight makes handling the reins easier for the rider, while the horse is encouraged to assume a proper head set without leaning on your hands.

HOLDING THE REINS

The reins can be held in several ways. Holding them in one hand is usually reserved for fully trained horses and experienced riders who have already learned to ride with a curb bit. One-handed riding is also used in neck reining where the horse reacts to the pressure of the outside rein against his neck.

The Rein Bridge

Start by forming a bridge with the reins held in both hands, as is usually done when training a young horse.

With the reins lying across your horse's neck, reach for them with both hands from above. It's not necessary to have the leather go through your middle and small finger. As pictured in the drawing, hold them very relaxed with slightly rotated wrists and carried in front of the saddle horn.

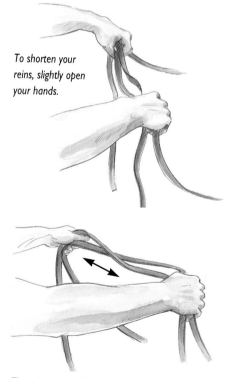

To shorten your reins, slightly open your hands.

The reins are lengthened by simply separating the rein bridge.

Sitting comfortably at a jog

MOVING ON

After you have found a correct and comfortable seat is the time to get your horse "in gear."

"WALK"

The aids used in Western riding are not very different from those in English style riding, except that you do not use constant pressure. You shift your weight slightly forward, at the same time giving with your hands. Even with loose reins, the horse will feel this aid. Apply pressure at the girth by the quick pressure of your lower legs and cluck your tongue or say "Walk." (Forget what you have learned about the "noble silence" of the dressage ring; vocal aids are acceptable here.)

If your horse does not react, repeat the aids in give-and-take fashion. Even if you have a particularly unmovable animal, give him only a few short but distinct taps with your legs and/or a short tap with a whip or the ends of the reins. Using constant pressure does nothing but dull a horse.

As soon as the horse walks off, relax your hands and back and take your legs away from his sides. Stay quiet, relaxed and passively in synch with the horse's motion. If he moves too slowly, give him a few encouraging taps with your legs. If he is obedient, leave him alone. The horse will continue to walk until you give him a new command.

As long as you go in a straight line, make sure that your weight is equally divided between both your seat bones.

TURNING

The next command will most likely be a change in direction. In the case of a well-schooled horse, a slight shift of your weight is usually enough—another reason why you must always sit straight in the saddle.

You have walked from the center of the ring to the fence and you would like to turn right. Just before you get to the track, shift your weight to the right and, if needed, apply light pressure with your left leg. Contrary to riding English dressage, you do not shorten the inside rein to lead a horse into a turn. You simply and very briefly apply a bit of pressure to initiate the correct direction, then immediately let the rein go slack again. At the same time, move your outside hand (here, the left) far enough to the inside so that rein touches the horse's neck. This neck-reining thereby "pushes" the horse to the inside. Keep the rein slack, with no sustained pressure to the mouth.

A Western horse turns in reaction to the shifting of his rider's weight and moves to the inside, away from the pressure of the outside rein and leg. As soon as you have reached the track, you assume your normal, centered seat and leave the horse alone.

by applying short, repeated impulses slightly behind the girth. Your inside leg remains on the girth. Continue with these aids until the horse assumes the desired position.

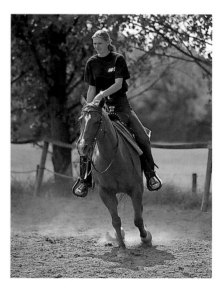

Tight Turns

To turn and make a circle, proceed as above. If you want to stay in the circle, simply keep contact with the outside rein and keep your weight shifted to the inside.

For tighter turns or to increase the bend, drive with your outside leg

Photos on the right: A right-hand turn, holding reins in both hands

Photo below: Turning with reins in one hand

The Jog or Light Trot

You use the same aids for "jogging" (the Western term for trotting) as for walking, only a little more forcefully. The voice command is "Jog." As soon as the horse obeys, discontinue all action on your part. If at first the horse jogs too fast, you might want to post. Since a Western saddle lacks knee rolls, posting requires you to be better balanced than if you were in an English saddle.

After a few times around the arena at this faster gait, slow the horse down by bracing your back and using your leg aids to drive his hindquarters under him. Support his head by holding the reins steady. Now the horse is jogging, which is a slow, even trot that looks almost as if the horse is dragging his feet. The suspension phase is reduced to a minimum, which is why this gait is so easy to sit to.

The Lope

Most Western horses go into the "lope," the Western term for canter, when they are given the so-called outside aids. These specific aids involve turning your horse slightly to the outside (meaning toward the rail), shifting your weight forward and somewhat to the outside, and driving with your outside leg while giving with the inside rein. That frees your horse's inside shoulder so he can take the correct lead.

Basically, the lope should be a collected canter with short but rhythmic and smooth strides.

The Western horse moves as if on padded hooves: the jog (above) is a collected trot, and the lope (below) like a quiet canter.

Western pioneer Jean Claude Dysli doing the sliding stop

"WHOA" MEANS "HALT"

Western riding does not use half-halts or halts, the way English riding does. Instead, it uses more or less constant holding aids with different amounts of pressure, depending on whether you want to shift into a lower gear or come to a full stop.

A voice command is particularly helpful because young Western horses have been taught during their training to react and come to a dead stop with a simple "Whoa" or some shortened version.

All you need do to stop is sink deep into the saddle and say the word. A well-trained horse will come to a complete stop even if you do nothing with the reins.

Activate the Hindquarters

To come to a stop from a walk in better balance, shift your weight slightly back by bracing your back and sitting deep—"sitting on your back pockets," to use a Western phrase. At the same time, apply slight pressure with the legs so that the horse is able to absorb the movement with his hindquarters. If his momentum shifts to his forehand, the horse will come to a slouching and unbalanced stop. In the event you move your hands slightly back and say "Whoa" but the horse only slows down and keeps going forward, repeat the aid more forcefully and add more rein action. Once you can get a stop from a walk, try it from a jog trot.

Speed

Increasing the tempo and letting the horse stretch his frame, as is customary in dressage, is not often done in Western riding. After all, Western gaits are comfortable for the rider and economical for the horse. A really fast lope is needed in ring work, for example, when the horse is about to make a spectacular sliding stop, but this maneuver should be done only by a very advanced rider and on a fully trained horse.

Changing Gaits

To make a transition from a lope to a jog, use the same aids. You'll learn over time how strong the application needs to be; it differs from horse to horse. The best way to learn is to experiment and practice. Use a forceful voice command only if you want to stop and because this is what the horse has been taught; if jogging or walking is what you want, simply call out "Jog" or "Walk."

REINING BACK

The reinback is accomplished by applying the aids for the halt. Shift your weight back, drive with both legs behind the girth and keep the reins steady. After the horse has completed a few steps backward, don't remain standing as is customary in dressage riding, but move forward immediately. Learning how to rein back at a faster tempo or when the horse is moving laterally will come later. Other advanced movements like flying lead changes, spins and roll-backs will also come in time—but by then you'll have outgrown this book.

DISMOUNTING

To dismount, come to a stop, take the slack reins in your left hand and grasp the saddle horn with your right. Swing your right leg back over and out of the saddle. Traditionalists keep their left foot in the stirrup until their right foot touches the ground.

Dysli and his Quarter Horse stallion performing a reinback

READY
FOR THE
TRAIL

Before you think about your first trail ride, we need to talk about how to test your riding skills. In addition, you should learn something about jumping, because on the trail you should be able to cope with a fallen tree or a ditch if necessary. After that, you'll be ready to leave the arena and capable of handling the world outside.

TESTING YOUR SKILLS

You may consider yourself a pretty good rider. After all, you've survived the first lesson on the lunge line, your backside and thigh muscles have grown accustomed to the saddle, and you no longer turn pale when the instructor gives the command to trot. Instead, you now find yourself gazing at those riders venturing outside the

The secret of being with horses is to be calm and to take your time.

ring and find yourself wishing, "Gee, I want to go, too."

First, a few suggestions. Ask your instructor's permission to work with the school horse you have been riding on a regular basis. Tell him you want to ride alone in the arena for an hour without an instructor or anyone else present. In other words, you want to make your first solo. For the first time, your horse will not hear the instructor's familiar and authoritarian voice, nor will he have the comfort of a four-legged companion behind or in front of him as he does during a group lesson.

EXPERIMENT

This is an opportunity for you to test what you have learned. All by yourself, try to ride the patterns and movements you have been taught during lessons. Change from a walk to a trot (or jog), halt, and trot again.

Don't be disappointed if everything doesn't go according to plan. For example, your leg aids may not be as well perfected as you thought, and your horse may balk at performing certain exercises. Horses are herd animals and riding in a group or under the command of the riding instructor is easier. Things often go well while you ride that way because the horse is clever enough to figure out what the instructor wants or what the other horses are doing.

Don't be discouraged if this first attempt doesn't live up to your expectations. Give yourself the gift of a few individual lessons and then try anoth-

Buffel: Alias Frustration

I don't remember how long I'd been riding, but it must have been at least a year. I had taken lessons at a stable that had excellent school horses. I thought I was good, and my riding instructor thought I "wasn't bad." That's why I was courageous enough to accept an invitation to join a friend and her horse on vacation. "Sure! Why not?"

I drove to her place and made friends with a gelding by the name of Buffel. Next morning came the moment of truth. Happily, I groomed and saddled my new friend and lead him to the empty riding arena. Obediently, he allowed me to mount.

Getting to the track at a walk presented no problem, but that was it! All attempts to move into a trot were futile. Everything I tried resulted in...nothing. Buffel clearly had no intention of trotting. I picked up a whip lying near the gate and gave him gentle tap on his behind. It was a mistake. It took more than ten minutes to slow him down, finally, to a walk after a spine-jarring trot.

I can't begin to say how crushed I was when I finally left the arena that day. But I began to understand the difference between riding under supervision on a trusted school horse in a group and being alone with a strange horse.

Experiences like that underscore the benefit of investing a few dollars for individual lessons. Look for chances to ride outside of your group lessons on unfamiliar horses. Adventures like the one I had are opportunities to learn.

Don't be afraid of jumping; it's usually not a big deal out on the trail.

er solo ride. You'll have learned what went wrong at your first solo try.

Your aids might not have been firm and clear enough. Remember, you need to know exactly what you want to do in order to convey that to your horse, and he needs to know that there is no room for discussion. Aids must be simple and precise, direct and unmistakable.

So far so good? Wonderful. Now you should make your first attempt at jumping.

LOW JUMPS

On the trail, you'll most likely come to a ditch or a fallen tree that you can't go around. So, you should be at least familiar with jumping, even if only on a beginning level, and not be afraid. Although most jumping is done using an English saddle, don't worry about it if you're riding Western style. There have been many times when cowboys needed their horses to take jumps, and small obstacles can also be jumped in a Western saddle.

Small hurdles are also easy to take in a Western saddle.

Start Low

The rule for jumping is the same as for all other riding activities: always start small. An obstacle one or two feet in height is handled the same way as a five-foot show jumping fence. If you've learned to jump and stay balanced without interfering with your horse's mouth, you can master anything in your path.

Wear Your Safety Helmet

Whether you ride English or Western, wear a safety helmet whenever you jump. That includes whenever you're out on a trail where low jumps are often a good possibility. In other words, a helmet is an absolute necessity on almost all occasions.

Shorten the Stirrups

If you are in an English saddle, you should shorten the stirrups by two or three holes, until the bottom of the irons strike the top of your ankle bones.

Practice the Light Seat

Jumping from a light two-point seat might not feel very comfortable in the beginning. Until you've found your balance, experiment by trotting or cantering a few times, lifting your seat slightly out of the saddle. The position relieves the horse's back of your weight and it's easier for you to stay in balance and then absorb the impact of landing after a jump. Federico Caprilli, one of the great riding masters at the beginning of the century, invented this "forward seat" style that revolutionized the sport.

It is important that you move in rhythm with the cantering horse. Jumping requires enormous flexibility in your foot, knee and hip joints, and close contact at the knees and long lower legs. Your foot should be further in the stirrups than usual during dressage riding. Your hands rest quietly and low alongside the horse's neck.

To assume the forward seat position, shorten the reins and "park" your hands on either side of the horse's neck. Go into a canter and keep your knees in firm contact with the saddle. Bend forward, elevating your seat slightly out of the saddle. Stand comfortably in the stirrups with steady lower legs and low heels. Canter a few times around the arena and ride a few circles. Then change to a trot and continue trotting in the same position.

THE FIRST JUMP

Your instructor will have built the first jump most likely along the long side of the arena. You'll have a quiet and experienced horse that you can rely on to do most of the work. Concentrate on your seat.

Approach the jump in a quiet trot. Assume the light seat and, depending on what your instructor requests, continue trotting or pick up a canter about thirty feet (10 meters) in front of the jump.

A CALM STRAIGHT-ON APPROACH

The approach to the jump should be as straight as possible. Position your horse so that he'll approach the jump in the exact center. Let the horse find his own tempo. The less you interfere the better, which means giving him enough rein. Don't "throw" the reins away, but a long rein is better than jarring the horse's mouth.

LIFT UP AND FORWARD

When your horse begins the jump, go with the movement and lift your seat slightly out of the saddle. Not too high, though: leave only enough air between your seat and the saddle so that, when the horse lands on the other side, you can gently sink back into the saddle. Over a low jump, you need only raise your seat as high as you do when you post to the trot.

Your knees are the hinges and anchor points. They should almost be glued to the saddle's knee rolls. A piece of paper held between the saddle and your knees should still be in place after you have completed your jump.

Your upper body is bent slightly forward from the hips, flexible enough so that your horse's thrust can close your hip angle. You may support your hands at the horse's neck (a tip from SLB: place your hands on the horse's crest with your knuckles against his neck for support). Once your horse has landed, assume again the original light seat.

When you have gained some experience, jump without your feet in the stirrups—an excellent exercise that will help you develop tight knee contact.

Riding with a light seat relieves the horse's back and your own seat.

The rider is "behind the movement," allowing too much weight to be shifted to the forehand.

Here, the rider is "ahead of the movement," again shifting the horse's weight too much to the forehand.

The rider is going "with the movement" and both rider and horse are in balance.

COMMON MISTAKES

• Ahead of the Movement

If you tend be ahead of the movement when anticipating a jump, you place too much weight on your horse's forehand. This prevents a fluid jump. Stay relaxed and don't anticipate the horse's leaving the ground. Stay balanced and don't try to help—it's the horse that does the jumping, not you. Let yourself be simply *carried* by the horse's movement.

• Behind the Movement

"Hanging behind" (also called "being left behind") causes you to remain in the saddle after the horse has left the ground. Then you find yourself off balance and leaning on the reins for support. More often than not, you'll "catch" the horse in the mouth. Many riders who are constantly left behind are timid or uncertain, and not quite ready to jump. Our advice here is also to relax, and perhaps grab a handful of mane. Then too, working over ground rails or low cavalettis will give you better balance and more assurance.

Two More Tips

Never interfere with your horse's mouth. Jumping is a favor that the horse is doing for *you* and he should be rewarded.

Never halt a horse in front of a jump. Horses can be taught to refuse that way. Nor should you slow down during the approach in the hope that jumping will be easier. All slowing down does is make things even worse. Instead, increase the pace, since most horses prefer to jump while they are moving faster.

JUMPING STYLE

Good style is not very important for a beginning jumper, but it won't hurt you to learn how to jump properly.

Correct form includes looking straight ahead at or beyond the jump, holding your back straight and your arms close to your sides and not sticking out. Your hands and reins are in one straight line to your horse's mouth. Your legs belong at or near the girth, with weight in your heels for support.

Ask your instructor to demonstrate good style. Others at your stable may be accomplished riders and you can watch what they do, or you can look at show jumping or eventing photographs in books and magazines, or on videotapes or television broadcasts of competitions.

Asking someone with a camera to videotape you in action after have taken a few jumping lessons will give you a clearer idea of your mistakes and what you need to work on. Concentrate on correcting one mistake at a time. For example, if you know you have a tendency to raise your hands during a jump, focus on fixing that problem. Once you have mastered your hand position, work on the position of your legs, and so forth. Like everything else, jumping must be practiced in order to acquire overall balance and a solid seat.

Ludger Beerbaum on It's Me demonstrates a perfect jump.

ON THE TRAIL

People can ride two abreast if a trail is wide enough. Riders keep a distance of one horse length in front and behind one another.

Your goal is in sight!

No matter how challenging, no dressage riding indoors or show jumping course can compare with being on the trail. For the authors, it has always been our ultimate goal. On the subject of trail riding, the book *Guidelines for Horseback Riding and Driving* says "Only when a rider has successfully managed his horse on a trail is he truly in control." Riding outdoors is without a doubt the most fun part of horseback riding.

FIRST, THE OUTDOOR ARENA

The first step is to take your horse to an outdoor arena. Get outside and into the fresh air. You'll quickly notice that your horse is suddenly more attentive. Even the oldest and most sluggish school horse becomes more alert and pays more attention to his surroundings. That shouldn't frighten you, though. Your ability to react will improve, becoming faster the more time you spend outdoors.

My First Outdoor Solo: Chamissa, or How I Learned What "XX" Means

It was a wonderful spring Sunday when I saw my friend Werner saddling his horse. "I'm going on a trail," he told me. I immediately thought: *I want to go, too.* My friend could obviously see what was on my mind and suggested I ask the stable manager if I could come along. Could I do this? Well, I'll never know unless I ask.

I found the manager who, after a moment's thought and head-scratching, said: "Sure, why not? Take Chamissa, since you know her."

I think I set a record in grooming and saddling.

A mere fifteen minutes later I proudly followed my friend Werner, Chamissa under me. I watched Werner's gelding stepping lively and thought to myself: "It won't hurt to have a quiet horse for the first outing, but did it have to be bone-lazy Chamissa?" That changed, though. I was perspiring before we ever reached the first little hill. When Werner began to trot, I had my hands full just to keep pace with him.

But it was wonderful. Crossing a bridge or a street presented no problem. Aside from the fact that we were jogging more than walking, Chamissa and I were having a good time, so much so that Werner suggested cantering up a hill.

I told him, "Please wait for me at the top." When I started to canter, in a light seat with tight knees and heels kept low, somebody woke up underneath me. Chamissa shot off like a rocket, passing my friend and taking the hill in long strides. For a moment I was stunned and wondered how it would end. But I quickly hit my stride, and it felt wonderful. I knew somehow that my horse was not running away, but simply coming alive.

We reached the top many lengths in front of my friend. The experienced Chamissa went back to a walk and turned around to look for Werner's horse.

When we returned to the stable, I told the boss how fast Chamissa was moving. He smiled knowingly and simply pointed to the name plate on her stall. There were two "X's" after the name of Chamissa's father. "XX stands for thoroughbred racehorse. It looks like, out on the trail, this little mare all of a sudden remembered..."

Stirrup Leather and Safety Helmet

For your first outing, ask your riding instructor to place a stirrup leather around your horse's neck. To quote again from *Guidelines for Horseback Riding and Driving*: "For trail riding we highly recommend placing a neck rein around the horse's neck. It's better horsemanship to reach for the neck rein when climbing and jumping than to hold onto the reins and catch the horse's mouth, causing him unnecessary pain."

You've heard the following before, but it bears repeating: A well-fitting safety helmet is a must when riding outside, either on a trail or in an outdoor arena.

We also recommend that you join a group for your first outing. With the leadership of your instructor, you can relax and enjoy yourself. He or she will make sure that the students and horses don't stampede off, and even those who have a tendency to get too exuberant will stay calm.

TAKE IT EASY

One reason why you learn to post is because that is how you trot in an English saddle on the trail. Cantering is always done with a light seat. Since the footing outdoors is rarely completely level, most horses move with greater unevenness than they do indoors, and riding with a light seat makes it easier for both horse and rider. However, you do sit back in the saddle for half-halts and changes of diagonals when posting.

Don't ride at the same speed over a long period of time, and only when the ground underneath is relatively soft. Your horse will thank you for it. When walking at leisure, give your horse a chance to stretch out his head and neck by giving him a long rein.

UPHILL AND DOWNHILL

Part of the attraction of trail riding is that, on a cross-country hack, a horse can keep on going when many all-terrain vehicles have to give up. A muddy track, where some vehicles will bog down, is only a small problem for a horse, who can deal effortlessly with a little creek or ditch. There are few mountains that an experienced rider cannot tackle on a horse. As long as a slope is not too steep, climbing is easily accomplished with a well-trained

Anke on Panthero riding downhill

horse. However, you might not want to tackle an Alp on your first outing.

To negotiate a hill, start practicing where you can choose the amount of incline. Begin at a walk or, to be more precise, at a speed that a sensible horse would use when nobody is in the saddle. Let the horse choose the tempo, but keep tight contact with your knees since some horses go uphill at a brisk canter.

It's your job to position your horse before negotiating a hill. Going up and coming down should be taken straight on in order to minimizing the danger of sliding.

Going Uphill

As you make sure your horse approaches a hill straight on, lean slightly forward and grasp the leather strap around your horse's neck. Assume a light seat and leave the reins passive. It's possible that your horse will approach and then climb a hill at a trot, which is his way to build up and then maintain forward movement. In most cases, he will settle down to a walk when he reaches the top.

Going Downhill

Going downhill is no different than going uphill, except that you might feel like leaning backward to stay in balance. Here, too, ride down straight and don't hold onto the reins. If your knees get weak, grab hold of the mane or neck strap with both hands for support.

Going uphill, Anke has assumed a light seat and thereby relieves Pantheros' back.

WATER: A MATTER OF TRUST

Some horses take crossing water in stride. They are unafraid and will simply proceed, no matter what kind of puddle or creek. Others, however, hesitate or have an outright fear of going through water. Don't get tough with such a horse when you are riding. Remember that resisting going into water is a perfectly natural instinct. Since horses cannot see the bottom of a stream or even a puddle, their instincts are telling them that dangerous objects might lurk underneath. Such horses are simply being cautious. Give them plenty of time, keep calm, and things will work out.

Preserve Your Leadership Position

But you still must cross the water. You don't want to make a wide circle every time and sometimes you couldn't even if you wanted to. You have no choice; you and your horse need to go through it. It becomes a matter of trust. Your horse will come to know that if you want to cross, it *must* be okay. Most of the time he'll simply march through if you use your aids firmly. Should he, however, doubt your leadership, he'll lose confidence. This is not only true when you come across a body of water, but for anything else that might be a problem on the trail.

The first order of business is to keep cool. If, every time you see a puddle, you think, *Oh no, he'll stop and we'll have a problem,* you'll clamp down your knees, and your horse will think, *What's happening? There must be something frightening ahead.*

A good trail rider is relaxed and approaches everything with a positive "we will make it" attitude. For a beginner, this attitude is difficult to come by. But when you are part of a group, simply place your trust in the leader. He or she won't get you into any dangerous situations, so you can just relax—and your horse will, too.

Exercise Patience

Don't discipline an easily frightened horse. Talk calmly, but remain firm in your resolve that you will now go through the puddle. It's *your* will that counts. You know there is nothing at the bottom of the puddle...no hoof-eating monster is waiting to attack. If *you* know that the ground underneath is solid, assume that your horse will walk through it. Emphasize your resolve by using your leg aids, speaking encouraging words and approaching the water straight on. If your horse still refuses, by either moving back or stepping sideways, turn him around and try again. Do this as long as it takes until he walks through. Sometimes you'll need a lot of patience. Usually, simply following the lead of another horse through the water is all that a reluctant animal needs to do.

JUMPING

No specific rules apply to jumping on the trail, other than to approach obstacles straight on and in a light seat so that your weight is off your horse's back. Don't interfere with his mouth. The pace of the horse and the aids you should use when approaching an obstacle depend on the type of jump, the condition of the ground and the temperament and training of the horse you're riding.

Trail riding is a matter of feeling. Every successful trail ride will bring new experiences and feelings of safety. If things sometimes do not work quite as well as you would hope, always remember: horses, too, have moods and good and bad days just as you do. The next day can be totally different. Never become discouraged, because ups and downs are part of horseback riding. They might even be the reason why being around your four-legged partner is so fascinating.

Urgen and the young son of Landeoso are performing a stylistically immaculate jump on the trail.

GLOSSARY

aids   devices and signals used to guide a horse: *natural*—indication from the rider's seat, legs, hands, voice; *artificial*—the bit, whip, spurs, etc.

bit   the metal piece of the bridle that fits into the horse's mouth, used to control the horse's speed and direction

bridle   the harness that fits over the horse's head

canter   a 3-beat gait that is also called a slow gallop

cavaletti   low barriers made of poles raised off the ground, used to train horses to jump

cinch   the leather strap that goes under the horse's belly and is buckled to secure the saddle; also, girth

collection   the compression-like shortening of a horse's stride

dressage   the systematic training of a horse; also a competition in which horses and riders execute predetermined patterns

fault   any of several types of penalties in jumper competitions, such as for knocking down a portion of the obstacle or refusing to jump an obstacle

flexion   the ability of a horse to "bend"; suppleness

forehand   the part of the horse in front of the saddle

gait   any of the movements at which a horse travels. Gaits are distinguished by the rhythm of their sequence of footfalls: walk (4 beat), trot (2 beat), and gallop and canter (3 beat).

gallop   a 3-beat gait faster than a canter; a horse's natural running movement

hand   the unit used to measure a horse's height; one hand equals 4 inches

hindquarters   the part of the horse behind the saddle

jog   a light, collected trot (Western)

lead   the sequence of footfall dur-ing the canter or gallop, as determined by whether the right or left leg strikes the ground first

lope   an easy canter (Western)

lunge or longe   working a horse in a circle, using a long line to guide the animal around the handler

posting   a method of riding at the trot, by raising and lowering oneself in the saddle according to the 2-beat gait

reinback   a use of the reins to back the horse, usually only three or four steps

reins   leather straps attached to the bit which are used to guide a horse

seat   a rider's position in the saddle

stirrups   metallic devices that accommodate the rider's feet. Hanging from each side of the saddle, they are used to mount and as support while riding.

supple   able to be easily flexed

tempo   rhythm as of movement; *see* gait

track   the area of the arena often "packed down" by the passage of horses, usually along the outer fencing; also, any path that a horse takes in an arena

transition   any change in gait or direction

trot   a 2-beat gait in which the horse's legs move in diagonal pairs

volte   a complete circle made on horseback

walk   the slowest of the horse's gaits, in a 4-beat rhythm

INDEX

CREDITS